• HALSGROVE DISCOVER SERIES ➤

Thomas Hardy's
DORSET

• HALSGROVE DISCOVER SERIES ➤

Thomas Hardy's
DORSET

Rodney Legg

HALSGROVE

First published in Great Britain in 2003, revised and expanded 2011

British Library Cataloguing-in-Publication Data
A CIP record for this title is available from the British Library

ISBN 978 0 85704 086 2

HALSGROVE
Halsgrove House,
Ryelands Business Park,
Bagley Road, Wellington, Somerset TA21 9PZ
Tel: 01823 653777   Fax: 01823 216796
email: sales@halsgrove.com

Part of the Halsgrove group of companies
Information on all Halsgrove titles is available at: www.halsgrove.com

Printed in China by Everbest Printing Co Ltd

Contents

Dedicated to Canon Edward Brooks of Fordington Vicarage
who was the first to ask me to write about Hardy

Introduction

WRITING ABOUT HARDY is exhilarating and exhausting. The first thing you realise from the extent of his work and many feet of shelf-space devoted to subsequent biographies is that he was an obsessively busy word-smith. That he won through, from a straw-roofed working class background, was due on one hand to perseverance and the other his initiative in developing new plots and subject matter in an evolutionary process rather than producing more of the same as his editors demanded. That would have secured his nineteenth-century financial security but not the enduring status of a world-class author. Having received the Order of Merit, and a visit by the Prince of Wales, he secured the admiration of the next generation of poets and novelists. He was never destined to be a great architect but he remains the only major British writer to design and build the house in which he wrote most of his work.

Hardy, having shaved off his beard, turned from novelist into poet

My aim has been to revisit the Dorset heartland of Hardy's Wessex as if with the author on a pre-car age exploration of its paths and byways. As with Hardy my first visits were usually by bicycle. In many cases his chosen places overlap my own both on the ground in Dorset and away, with the coincidence that I also had grandparents living near Reading, and went through brief flirtations with London life and work. Wareham and its branch of the Hardy family are my roots though the accident of a Bournemouth birth tends to spoil the credentials.

Tom Hardy gives all the right reasons for returning home. His literary locations were told to Hermann Lea and have been added to by James Stevens Cox - some personally after he ordered a 'steak, rare, with ice-cream' - and authors Denys Kay-Robinson and Fred Pitfield. Personal revisions plus another score, several since recycled by other authors, have been my contribution to the game. Some 550 are listed in a glossary after the main text.

This book had its origins in visits to Canon Edward Brooks at Fordington Vicarage. Having asked me to write a feature for the Official Handbook of the Thomas Hardy

Festival, in 1968, he later passed on his own anecdotes. The best, which I shall put into its 1907 context in the relevant chapter, concerns how Mrs Florence Hardy came to meet her husband: 'I was introduced to mine by Dracula!'

Some documents which belonged to the Moule family of Fordington, nearly a century earlier, were given to me by Tom Perrott of Bridport who chaired the Ghost Club in London. Roland Gant, who edited and published Hardy's revealing two volume biography by Robert Gittings, sent me researching other possibilities. Eric and Anna Winchcombe, custodians of Hardy's Cottage birthplace, provided the counter-blast to the opinions of Gittings and Gant, not to mention a barrage of bizarre theories from Lois Deacon who was sure that Hardy had fathered an illegitimate son by his cousin Tryphena Sparks. I left my mark on the living room by finding the old iron chimney-crooks that now hang in the fireplace at Hardy's birthplace.

Here I try to give a balanced view of Hardy and his relations and a dispassionate reappraisal of his overlapping affairs with Emma and Florence. There is much more that could be written about Emma's dedication to the anti-vivisection cause and Florence's later social work for Mill Street Housing Society. Not all you are going to read has come from published biographies. Here be other ghosts.

Chapter One
Monument to the other Thomas

THROUGH DESCENT FROM the Wareham branch of the Hardy family I acquired a miniature Regency gold and sapphire brooch, containing a lock of fair hair from a queue, or pony tail as we know it. With it came a hand-written note in blotted ink on aged and stained paper. This reads, in the original spelling:

'A locett of the hare of Lord Nelson gived to my husband by Admirel Hardy for his loyal servis. Jane Long, W. Millton.'

Vice-Admiral Sir Thomas
Masterman Hardy

Left: Admiral Hardy gave a lock of Nelson's hair to a servant

The west Dorset hamlet of West Milton, in the parish of Powerstock, lay across the hills from the Admiral's home. The note was pinned to a copy of *The Times* for Friday January 10, 1806 which carries a large print of a coffin and the heading 'Funeral of Lord Nelson'. The mementoes are accompanied by a small cube of dark oak with a copper plate inscribed "Piece of HMS *Victory*, 1886".

Thomas Hardy, the novelist, was between four and six years old when a new landmark gradually arose on the western horizon. It was clearly visible from the window seat in his cottage bedroom at Higher Bockhampton when he grew up in Cherry Lane which was locally known as Veterans Alley. Though the Nelsonian memento came to me via reclusive relative George Hardy, I have a direct link with Hardy's home parish in that my paternal 2nd great-grandparents (James Legg and wife Esther Hurst) lived at Lower

Bockhampton. They appear on the next page of the 1841 census return from the entry for baby Thomas Hardy.

His immediate neighbours were the old soldiers and sailors of the Napoleonic Wars that took place a generation earlier. The landmark, which would be likened to 'a factory chimney' by Sir Frederick Treves, was for Nelson's flag-captain at the Battle of Trafalgar of 'Kiss me, Hardy' fame. Our notable common ancestor - for the Hardys of Portesham and, Stinsford and my own Hardy relatives at Wareham - was Thomas Hardye of Frampton who founded the Grammar School in South Street, Dorchester, in 1569.

Thomas Masterman Hardy has been immortalised by Horatio Nelson's dying words. These will inevitably attract correspondence, even now, because they always do. The Nelson Society, and just about all historians who have looked in detail at his life and times, agree that he did say those words. Mr Beatty, the Victory's surgeon, and Dr Scott, the chaplain, both confirmed that Nelson said 'Kiss me, Hardy' as he died in his arms on HMS Victory at the Battle of Cape Trafalgar on 21 October 1805.

However, as at least a dozen correspondents are now in the process of telling me, revisionist Victorians insist that the words he actually used were 'Kismet, Hardy'. That accords with our received notions of traditional British reserve of how the nation's greatest naval hero should have phrased his language. The problem is that the Turkish word for fate and destiny, which would then have been rendered as kismat in its original Arabic form, was not current in the western world until later in the nineteenth century. So, we have to come to terms with Nelson's words as human and moving, as Georgian society did at the time.

Lord Nelson's favourite captain and companion in battle became Vice-Admiral Sir Thomas Masterman Hardy. The second son of Joseph Hardy, of Portesham, he was born at Kingston Russell House on 15 April 1769. He went from active service to the Governorship of Greenwich Hospital, being appointed on 6 April 1834, where he did much to improve the lot of the 2,000 naval pensioners who lived in the hospital and Royal Naval College. He died in the Second Sea Lord's house at Greenwich on 20 September 1839 and his coffin lay in the dining room before burial in Greenwich Mausoleum.

By 1843, there was a determination to provide a Dorset memorial, and the sum of £609-15s-0d had been raised by the public subscription among the gentry to commemorate his distinguished life. It was decided to erect a Gothic column on Black Down. This commanding peak lies in the triangle between the Hardy family's homes, at Kingston

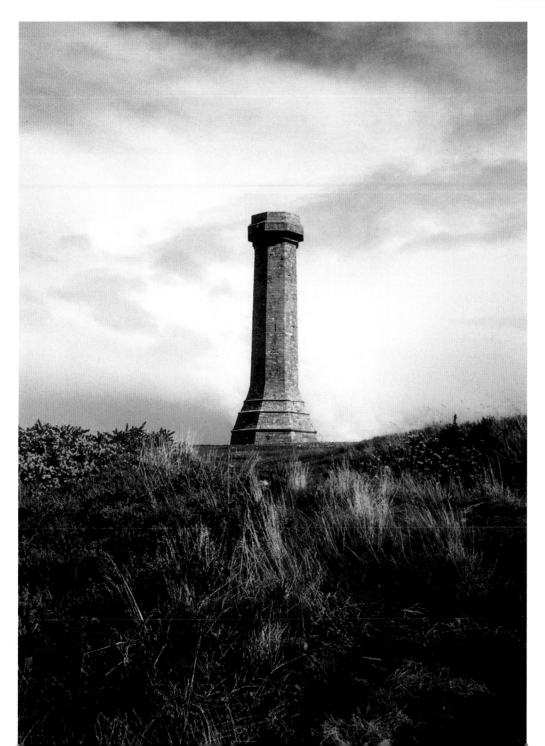

The Hardy Monument rose from the heather and gorse when novelist Thomas was a boy

Russell, Martinstown and Portesham, with an appropriately sweeping view over Weymouth and Portland to the shipping in the English Channel.

The monument was designed by Arthur Dyke-Troyte. Its first stone was laid in 1844 by Mrs Floyer, wife of John Floyer, MP for Dorset and High Sheriff of the county. The contract price to Mr Goddard, the builder, was £375-19s-6d; for opening quarries at Portesham and quarrying stone, £111-13s-3d; to Mr Glegg and Mr H. Barnes for submitting designs, £5 each; advertisements for donations, £33-10s-11d; for beer £6-1s-8d and £2-19s-8d for bread and cheese, for the work people on the occasion of laying the foundation stone.

Below left: *Coastal view, looking across Weymouth's hinterland, to Portland*

Below right: *Scaffold-clad, for winter repairs by the National Trust, to make the tower safe*

The base of the tower is at 786 feet above the level of the sea, to an octagonal design which inclines inwards like the batter of a mediaeval castle - from a base which is 28 feet in diameter - into parallel sides with a flared top for the viewing platform. Here the building reaches 72 feet, making a total height of 858 feet. A circular staircase winds up the middle, around the central pillar, and is sparsely lit by narrow slit-windows. From its prominent position it may be seen in every direction, and in clear weather at a considerable distance, from Purbeck and the Isle of Wight eastwards and from Start Point and Dartmoor westward. It is also a conspicuous object to vessels passing up and down the English Channel, as well as to all the surrounding country.

In 1901, W. Hardy Manfield of Portesham House, representing the descendants of Vice-Admiral Sir Thomas Hardy, leased the Hardy Monument to the new National Trust for Places of Historic Interest or Natural Beauty, which was founded in 1895. The landmark had been restored in 1900 as a result of initiatives largely funded by Colonel Robert Williams MP, whose country seat was Bridehead, in the delightful valley at Littlebredy. It was the Trust's first Dorset property - leasehold, that is - with the first freehold property being the Cerne Giant hill-figure.

Another hero was commemorated on the hilltop in 1920. A stone seat was erected on the seaward side of the Hardy Monument as a memorial to Major William Digby Oswald who was killed on the Somme, at the age of 36 on 16 July 1916, by the shell-band from a British gun which fired prematurely. A 'soldier's soldier', Oswald had seen action behind enemy lines and was a veteran of the Boer War, Natal rebellion, and Zulu rising. He was buried on the Somme, at Dives Copse near Bray, but his comrades decided upon an English memorial, overlooking the Weymouth countryside where he had met his wife, Catherine Yardley.

At sea, the Hardy name would have a distinguished war record, being carried by a 1936-built destroyer of 1,505 tons which was commanded by Captain Bernard Warburton-Lee in a defiant action against German vessels invading Norway, at Narvik on 10 April 1940. HMS *Hardy* was lost in a courageous action which won Warburton-Lee a posthumous Victoria Cross. A tribute was attached to the door of the Hardy Monument from the people of 'Possum' (the local name for Portesham):

'Nelson's Hardy and Hardy's Possum salute you.'

The replacement vessel that took the famous name, commissioned in 1943, was the flagship of the Royal Navy's 26th Destroyer Flotilla. This *Hardy* was sunk by a German

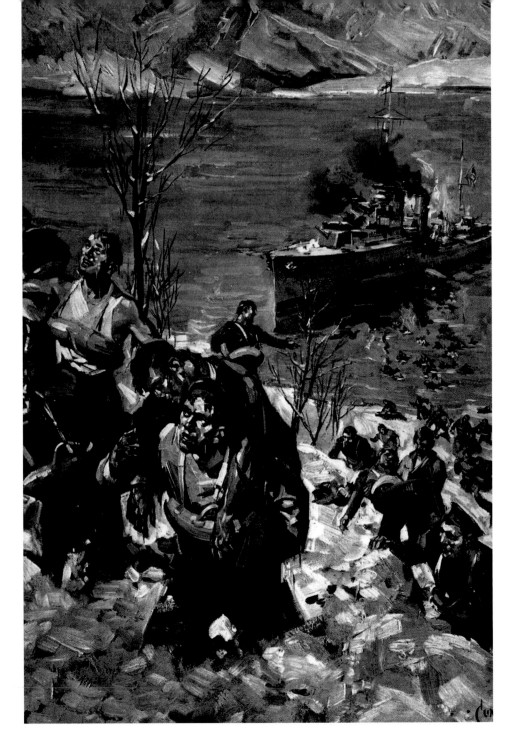

'Hardy' *heroism at Narvick in 1940*

The destroyer HMS Hardy
had a short war

homing torpedo whilst escorting an Arctic convoy, towards northern Russia, on 30 January 1944. Forty men were lost. 'Captain D', sailing in her as commander of the flotilla, survived and would retire as Vice-Admiral Sir Geoffrey Robson.

In 1938 the National Trust acquired the freehold of the Hardy Monument and purchased three-quarters of an acre of the hilltop. Colonel Sir Robert Williams provided a fund for maintenance. Its car-park and the surrounding slopes are owned by the Duke family of Maiden Newton. This open expanse of windswept vegetation is designated by English Nature as a site of special scientific interest, for its clumps of heather, gorse and wild bilberries, on the acidic gravel soil which caps the underlying chalk.

It is truly the heart of the Hardy Country. Explaining that to visitors has become ever harder as Thomas One is now totally eclipsed by Thomas Two. The latter was fascinated by astronomical spectacles and would be delighted that Hardy Monument is now the choice venue for witnessing cosmic events. It offers the widest of dark skies, in theory, though the hill-fog of reality is often as opaque as the mists of fiction. For often the Hardy Monument is literally invisible and bears out a popular Dorchester saying that predicts the weather. If you can see it, it is going to rain - when you can't, then it's already raining.

Chapter Two
Childhood at Bockhampton

OUR THOMAS HARDY (1840-1928) came into the world in the cob-and-thatch cottage at Higher Bockhampton of a jobbing builder and his extended family. He appeared as a frailty, whom the nurse feared was dying, in the central room upstairs above the living room. This was the parental bedroom. His father was Thomas Hardy (1811-92) and his grandfather was Thomas Hardy (1778-1837). Their house was built by great-grandfather

The Rhododendron Mile across Puddletown Heath

'The Birthplace' as Tom Hardy knew it

The piercing eye of great-aunt Sarah Swetman from Tolpuddle was a presence in the house

John Hardy (1756-1822), in about 1800, on an acre of land at the end of a sandy lane, leased from the Morton Pitt family of Kingston Maurward, backing on to the heath that extended to Puddletown Beacon and Puddletown village. John's grandson, Thomas Hardy senior, made Jemima Hand (1813-1904) pregnant. She was a cook in domestic service.

They married at Melbury Osmond, near Yetminster, on 22 December 1839. Thomas Hardy junior was born on 2 June 1840 in Hardy's Cottage - 'The Birthplace' - which is now opened to the public by the National Trust. Because he was a delicate baby, aunt Mary Hann came to live at Bockhampton, in the parish of Stinsford to the east of Dorchester, to help look after Tom, as he was always known, after his sister Mary was born. That was on 23 December 1841 and aunt Mary stayed till her marriage to John Antell of Puddletown in 1847.

Tom's paternal grandmother, Mary Head Hardy from Fawley, Berkshire, also lived in the modest creeper-clad building which Hardy memorably described as a 'a one-eyed blinkin' sort of place'. In a bedroom, Irene Cooper Willis tells us, there was the 'All-seeing

Eye' of a portrait in oils of great-aunt Sarah Swetman from Tolpuddle, in her black widow's weeds of a generation earlier. Painted at the age of 76, in 1832, she was stern and brown-eyed with Tom's hooked nose. His paternal great-grandmother, Betsy Swetman, also came from Tolpuddle.

Stinsford's early eighteenth-century white marble font in which baby Tom was baptised is now in St Lukes' church, Stanmore, Winchester, having been replaced in 1920 by its displaced Norman predecessor which Hardy rediscovered in the churchyard.

By the age of seven Tom was not only reading serious books but played the accordion and could tune a fiddle. His father introduced him to country dance music and the hymns of Isaac Watt, which until 1842 he had played for the choir in St Michael's parish church, at Stinsford. Father and son played together at wedding receptions and country house dances. Over in Puddletown, his aunt Martha Hann married George Brereton Sharpe, in 1841. An ex-Lancer, Sharpe became a farm manager for Lord Salisbury on the Hatfield Estate, and provided the model for Sergeant Francis Troy in *Far From the Madding Crowd*.

As a young child, Tom watched the building of the Southampton and Dorchester Railway across the meadows a mile-and-a-half from his home, between West Stafford and

Garden view of Hardy's Cottage with upstairs windows being those of the birth-room (above door) *and young Thomas Hardy's bedroom* (right)

North-east corner of Hardy's Cottage, from Snail Creep path, with visitors at the American monument (left)

THOMAS HARDY'S DORSET

The Lodge in Yellowham Wood provided the setting for Under the Greenwood Tree

The parents' central bedroom at Hardy's Cottage where Thomas was born on 2 June 1840

Hardy's bedroom, towards the southern end of Hardy's Cottage, with the window seat where Under the Greenwood Tree *was written*

20

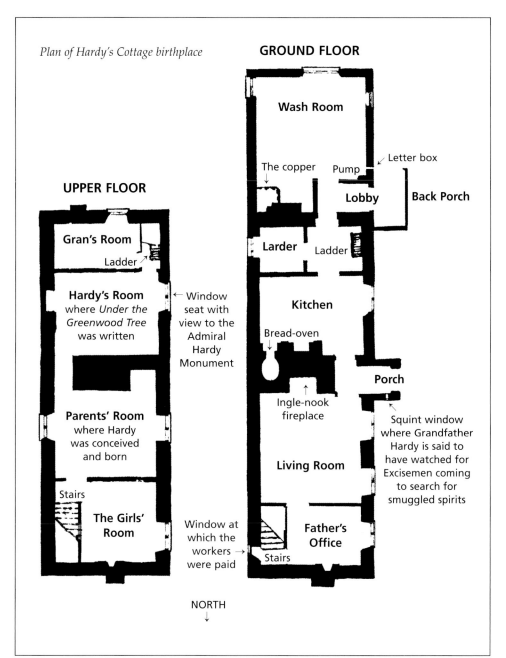

Plan of Hardy's Cottage birthplace

GROUND FLOOR

Wash Room

The copper

Pump

← Letter box

Lobby

Back Porch

Larder

Ladder

Kitchen

Bread-oven

Porch

Ingle-nook fireplace

Squint window where Grandfather Hardy is said to have watched for Excisemen coming to search for smuggled spirits

Living Room

Window at which the workers were paid

Father's Office

Stairs

NORTH
↓

UPPER FLOOR

Gran's Room

Ladder

Hardy's Room
where *Under the Greenwood Tree* was written

← Window seat with view to the Admiral Hardy Monument

Parents' Room
where Hardy was conceived and born

Stairs

The Girls' Room

The girls' northern bedroom at Hardy's Cottage

The living room downstairs in Hardy's Cottage

Fordington. It opened into the county town on the day before his birthday in 1847. His was to be the generation that saw the arrival of the train, the motor car and the aeroplane (not that he ever flew), plus photography, the telephone and the machine-gun.

Tom Hardy's formal education began in 1848 at the Church of England National School provided in Lower Bockhampton by landowner's wife Julia Augusta Martin from Kingston Maurward House. Childless herself, she adopted Tom as her pet pupil, cuddling and kissing him. Perhaps because of that, Tom was removed to Isaac Glanfield Last's Nonconformist British School in the Greyhound Yard, Dorchester, in 1850. Decades later an old man captured this vignette of young Tom for the essayist Llewelyn Powys:

'I can see 'en now, a little nipper going off to school with a bag all a-coloured like Jacob's jacket.'

Entering Dorchester, he passed through Fordington, where a cholera epidemic raged, and Revd Henry Moule held the Duchy of Cornwall to account for deplorable living conditions. Tom wrote to Handley Moule - the Bishop of Durham - in 1919:

'I well remember the cholera years in Fordington; you might have added many details. For instance, every morning a man used to wheel the clothing and bed-linen of those who had died during the night, out into the mead, where the Vicar had a large copper set. Some was boiled there and some was burnt. He also had large fires kindled in Mill Street to carry off the infection.'

Despite poor handwriting, Tom remained teacher's pet, and was spared the usual discipline because of his academic prowess. By 1852, as the family's building business recovered from the Hungry Forties, Latin was added to the curriculum at an additional charge which they were now able to pay. Hardy devised his own visual recognition system for remembering genders. His average daily walk, to and from the centre of Dorchester, was 5 miles.

Isaac Last founded his own Academy in 1853 and Tom continued to be his star pupil.

By now the family at Bockhampton had grown, with brother Henry being born on 1 July 1851 and sister Katharine - known as Kate or Katie - following in 1856. Tom continued to have his head in books and journals, on which he spent all his pocket-money, and shunned the company of other boys. In 1854 he had the first of his infatuations with an attractive girl,

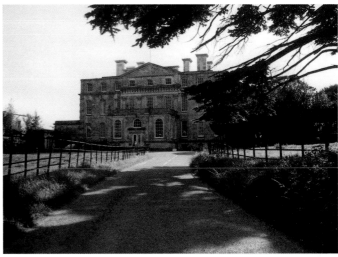

Above left: Stinsford House and the parish church in 1857

Above right: 'The big house' at Kingston Maurward was the home of Mrs Julia Augusta Martin

The south front of Stinsford House before renovation

St Michael's parish church,
no longer ivy-clad, from the
south-east

The music gallery in Stinsford
church was replaced in 1996

merely glimpsed on horseback, of the safe-sex kind that would transfer to actresses playing his *Tess of the d'Urbervilles* in later life. Another, red-haired gamekeeper's daughter Elizabeth Bishop, would be immortalised in the poem 'To Lizbie Browne'. Hardy's observations of young ladies also gave him many of the originals for characters in his novels. He confessed to 'immaturity' caused by 'lateness of development in virility'.

Things came to a head in his assault on elder cousin Rebecca Sparks, while both were drunk at a Christmas Mummers' rehearsal in 1855, as a result of which he was told not to return to Puddletown. Head-strong Rebecca was quite capable of looking after herself. She would prove that by marrying Frederick Paine and then leaving him immediately. The wedding ceremony finished with a blazing row and Rebecca walked out on Frederick as he stood bewildered at the door of Puddletown church. As Hardy would observe, through Sergeant Troy in *Far From the Madding Crowd* after his wedding in that very church, 'a ceremony before a priest doesn't make a marriage'.

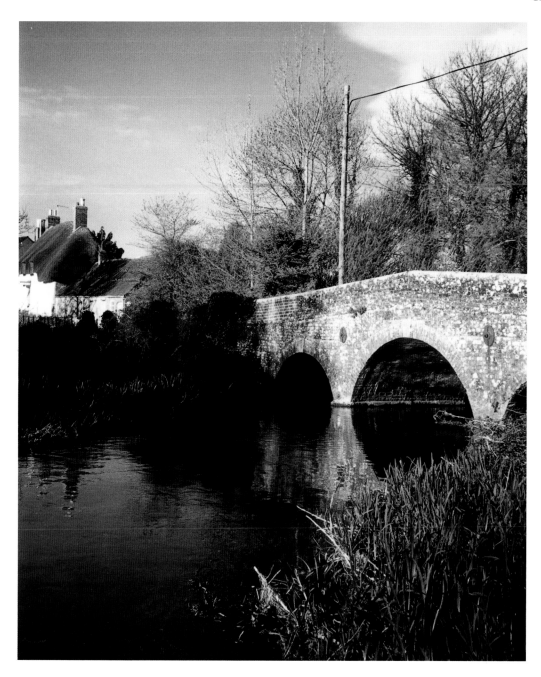

Humped bridge over an arm of the River Frome between Lower Bockhampton and the water-meadows

The fifteenth-century church has survived, mediaeval and magnificent, complete with dark oak pews and a large gallery where musicians played at services until 1845. Puddletown and its volatile Sparks family provided Hardy with the best of settings and stories. These were full of incident and emotion. Without the wealth of material that came from this working class background - which he spent a lifetime concealing - he may well have never progressed beyond a mere purveyor of ponderous prose and pedantic poetry.

Hardy himself realised this when he admitted that Weatherbury folk were:

'. . . by no means uninteresting, intrinsically. If report spoke truly, they were as hardy, merry, thriving, wicked a set as any in the whole country.'

Stinsford village and flock from the main road into Dorchester

Chapter Three
Architect turns Author

AS YOUTHS, BROTHERS Tom and Henry embarked on a tour of the cathedral cities of southern England. They travelled on their Sunbeam bicycles and put up for the nights in village inns. Thomas's very restrained tipple was ginger-beer shandy.

In his self-revelatory poem 'Wessex Heights' of 1896, Tom implies that as a 16-year-old in 1856 he considered becoming a clergyman but 'cannot go to the tall-spired town, being barred by the forms now passed'. Salisbury had the diocesan theological college and such a rejection, Professor J. O. Bailey argues in *The Poetry of Thomas Hardy*, would have marked a turning-point in his life. He writes that Dr Elsie Smith, the librarian at Salisbury, 'discovered correspondence indicating Hardy's application to prepare himself for the

Woodsford Castle, measuring up of which in 1856 started the career of Thomas Hardy, architect

Right: *Hardy's first published work was the press release for the renovation of St Peter's church in Dorchester*

Far right: *Hardy's font, designed for Coombe Keynes parish church, is now at Wool*

Martha Brown's crime of passion was committed at Birdsmoor Gate, Marshwood

Church and his rejection by the authorities'. Similarly, the main character in *Jude the Obscure*, his most autobiographical novel, is turned away from Oxford.

Thomas Hardy senior worked for Dorchester architect John Hicks on the restoration of Woodsford Castle. Thomas junior was asked to help measure it for the plans. Hicks was impressed enough to offer an apprenticeship and 16-year-old Tom Hardy reported for work in the draughtsman's office at 39 South Street, Dorchester, in July 1856. Hardy's first published work, a deadly dull press release for the local newspaper, described the renovation of St Peter's church, Dorchester, in 1856-57. He may also have contributed articles to *The Dorset County Chronicle* on similar projects at Rampisham, Powerstock, Bridport, Coombe Keynes and new Gothic churches provided for Athelhampton and Bettiscombe in 1862. Drawings for the font at Coombe Keynes - dated 8 April 1861 - show it is Hardy's work, though to see it you now have to visit Holy Rood church at Wool, since the parish church at Coombe Keynes was declared redundant.

In Dorchester on 9 August 1856, Tom had one of life's pivotal experiences which resonated through his work, and still preyed on his mind in old age. Martha Brown of Birdsmoor Gate, Marshwood, had found her husband, John, in the act of making love to Mary Davies. In the row that followed John hit Martha with his carter's whip. She retaliated with a hatchet in the ultimate crime of passion - for which she was sentenced to death. The hanging was in public from the 'New Drop' over the low stone arch into the County Gaol in North Square, Dorchester.

Hardy had one of the best views as a crowd of 4,000 gathered to watch. Revd Henry Moule, vicar of Fordington, accompanied her to the scaffold because the prison chaplain, Dacre Clemetson, was too distraught to appear. Martha, however, maintained her

Revd Henry Moule, vicar of Fordington, accompanied Martha Brown to the scaffold

composure. With delicate dignity, in a thin black gown in the damp morning air, her soft features became moulded by the drizzle into a marble-like stiffness, making an indelible impression on Tom Hardy. The judicial death of Martha Brown stirred the imagination for what he turned into his series of Wessex tragedies. He also watched, through a telescope from Rainbarrows on the heath above Bockhampton, the execution of 19-year-old James Searle on 10 August 1858. He had killed Sarah Ann Guppy, a 'deformed and diminutive' young woman, in an unprovoked attack at Stoke Abbott.

Tom's brother, Henry, was set to follow the family trade as a builder. The elder of their two sisters, Mary, several cousins, and other friends were dispersing in search of work. Emma Sparks, another of his Puddletown cousins, emigrated and died in Queensland. Favourite aunt Martha Sharpe suffered the same fate in Ontario. Fellow apprentice Henry Robert Bastow had gone to Tasmania. Another young acquaintance, Thomas William Hooper

Public executions, witnessed as a teenager, had a lifelong impact on Hardy's writings

Tolbort, entered the Indian Civil Service. Their mutual friend and mentor Horace, christened Horatio Moseley Moule - a brilliant but clinically depressed son of Fordington's vicar - urged Thomas Hardy to take the obvious next step in his chosen profession and make his fortune in the Empire's booming capital.

Tom Hardy visited Salisbury Cathedral as an architect's pupil, in a 'driving mist' in 1860, when James Wyatt's 'improvements' of 1792 had begun to age and changes were mooted. The problems were beyond the scope of a provincial practice. There was diocesan concern about the stability of the spire, leading to George G. Scott and F. W. Sheilds being commissioned to report on 'The Tower and its Sustaining Piers'.

John Hick's senior pupil, Fippard, had been returning from London talking of the excitement of the Cremorne and Argyle dance-halls, and proved his point by cavorting around the office floor with an imaginary partner, humming the tune of a quadrille. Peer pressure seems to have had its effect.

Hardy the architect, studious at twenty-one in 1861

Hardy moved to London, into lodgings at 3 Clarence Place, Kilburn, on Thursday 17 April 1862. He had a return ticket, back to Dorchester Station, and made the rounds of architects looking for work. He might have had to use the ticket, had it not been for a chance remark, that Arthur Blomfield needed a young Gothic draughtsman to design churches and rectories. He was the son of a bishop, whose brother was also one, so ecclesiastical faculties were a family preoccupation. Hardy fitted the bill and reported to the drawing-office at 9 St Martin's Place, Trafalgar Square, on 5 May 1862.

'Any spice in the papers?' was Blomfield's customary morning greeting. Hardy fitted in well with his peers - 'Tory and Churchy' - and joined in their japes against radicals and reformers. Hardy's vision was backwards to Dorset rather than forward into the political future. Bar an abiding fascination in public executions, his notes and letters show hardly any interest in national or world events, but that applies to most young men in any era.

Tom frequented coffee-houses and galleries. He attended Covent Garden Opera House as well as the dance-rooms, saw Shakespearean actor Charles John Kean perform, and listened to a reading by Charles Dickens. His musical side came to the fore, with office sing-songs, followed by evening duos with Tom on an old fiddle and a colleague at the piano. There was a brief reunion with Julia Martin of Kingston Maurward, who had also moved to London, but she found a 22-year-old man lacked the allure of the little boy she adored. They never met again.

On 21 November 1863, Tom accompanied Blomfield at the laying of the foundation stone by the Princess Royal at All Saints' church in New Windsor. 'Take it, take it!' she said, handing the commemorative trowel back to Blomfield, having smeared her gloves with mortar.

In 1863, Blomfield's office moved to 8 Adelphi Terrace, overlooking the Thames from Adam Street in the Strand. Hardy lodged at 16 Westbourne Park Villas, Bayswater, near Paddington Station. His 'Essay on Coloured Bricks and Terra-cotta Architecture' won him a prize from the Institute of British Architects in 1863. 'How I Built Myself a House', an article in *Chamber's Journal* on 18 March 1865, was Thomas Hardy's first paid work to be published. It earned him £3-15s-0d. That was the average agricultural wage in Dorset for a full month's work.

Despite this footing in his chosen profession, he was feeling depressed on 2 June, as his diary entry shows:

'My 25th birthday. Not very cheerful. Feel as if I had lived a long time and done very little. Walked about by moonlight in the evening. Wondered what woman, if any, I should be thinking about in five years' time.'

On 27 October 1865, Arthur Blomfield with employees Hardy and Lee attended the state funeral of Lord Palmerston, in Westminster Abbey. Blomfield, with his nose for gossip, would have relished the story that Palmerston was the first British Prime Minister to die whilst making love to his mistress. The event is said to have taken place on the billiard table.

Hardy's coastal diversion of the mid-1860s was to Kimmeridge Bay and its Clavell Tower with coastguard's daughter Eliza Nicholls

Tom Hardy was also enjoying an emotional fling, with Eliza Nicholls, whose father had served at Kimmeridge Coastguard Station. She was a maid, to a barrister's wife in Westbourne Park Villas, where Hardy had moved in the summer of 1863. Eliza moved to Findon, Sussex, where her father was now stationed, and Hardy also had an infatuation with her younger sister, Mary Jane Nicholls. The affair was over by the middle of 1867 when Hardy penned a poem of regret, 'Neutral Tones'.

His health and mental state were suffering so he decided to leave London and return home to Dorchester. This coincided with his old job being available. John Hicks, now also ill, wanted him back.

Home again, at Bockhampton, Tom started work on his first novel in August 1867. The first draft of *The Poor Man and the Lady* was completed in January 1868. Hardy was applying all his spare time to writing - at the rate of 20 manuscript pages a week - with the physical result that he soon sported a beard. Though encouraged by publisher Alexander Macmillan and editor John Morley he withdrew the book while it was awaiting judgement from a second reader. It was then turned down by Frederick Chapman of Chapman and Hall, followed by William Tinsley of Tinsley Brothers, though the latter offered to reconsider if the author would pay towards publication.

Hicks died on 12 February 1869 and his work, together with Hardy, was taken over by George Crickmay of Weymouth. Work in progress included the rebuilding of Turnworth parish church for rich widow Julia Parry-Okeden in memory of husband William. Hardy drew the tracery details of birds, leaves and flowers for the capitals on the columns, plus corbels of bearded heads and an owl. The latter, a rather twee Hamstone carving inside the tower, was ornithologically topical as the bird had only recently begun breeding in central southern England. The species had arrived in Kent - from Flanders - a decade earlier.

Mrs Parry-Okeden's home, Turnworth House, provided the original for Hintock House in *The Woodlanders*.

The Dorchester drawing office was closed and Hardy worked from Weymouth where the office was at 77 St Thomas Street. He lodged at 3 Wooperton Street, a three-storey Victorian terrace house with a bay-window overhanging the pavement, and a view over Radipole Lake towards the Hardy Monument.

Hardy threw his literary efforts into the melodrama *Desperate Remedies*, daring and erotic, which has the lady of Knapwater House in bed with her maid, perhaps because Hardy imagined the real-life house and owner, Kingston Maurward and Julia Martin who used to cuddle him as a child. In a 'smouldering passion' the maid dresses her with 'silk

Work at Turnworth parish church (centre left) *provided a prime rural location*

Turnworth House, the home of Mrs Julia Parry-Okeden, provided the original for Hintock House in The Woodlanders

Hardy restored Turnworth church in 1869

Hardy's little owl at Turnworth

stockings and white shoes'. Havelock Ellis, in his *Studies of the Psychology of Sex*, noted that Hardy showed 'an unusual but by no means predominant interest in the feet and shoes of his heroines'.

The Dorset County Chronicle of 28 October 1869 conveniently provided the description of a fire which devastated buildings at Athelhampton which is put to dramatic use. In February 1870, after cousin Tryphena Sparks - Triffie, with whom he may have been emotionally entangled - left Dorset for Stockwell Training College for Schoolmistresses in South London, Hardy quit his Weymouth lodgings and went home to Bockhampton. His sister Mary had also returned, after leaving college, via a teaching assignment at Dogbury Gate, Minterne Magna. She was now employed across the hill in Piddlehinton School. Younger sister Kate, 13-years-old, would soon finish her schooling.

The final church commission inherited from John Hicks saw Hardy heading west in the early hours of 7 March 1870 - by foot and then trains - to Launceston, Cornwall. He went onwards by trap to St Juliot, near Boscastle, on the Atlantic coast. Here, that Monday evening, he was shown into the drawing-room in the Rectory, to be met by a blue-eyed blonde. 'Received by young lady in brown,' he wrote. She was 29-year-old Miss Emma Lavinia Gifford. Born in Plymouth, on 24 November 1840, she was just a few months younger than Tom. Emma's elder sister, Helen Gifford, had married the widowed rector of St Juliot, Revd Caddell Holder.

Hardy's expenses, refunded by Crickmay on 12 March, totalled £6-10s-9d. It was an investment that bought him a wife.

As a writer, Emma's suitor had formidable hurdles to overcome, in London's publishing establishment. *Desperate Remedies* was also rejected by Alexander Macmillan and John Morley. It was ruined, Morley wrote to Macmillan, 'by the disgusting and absurd outrage which is the key to its mystery - the violation of a young woman at an evening party, and the subsequent birth of a child'. Whether it was 'too abominable to be tolerated' we cannot say as the offending scene was removed at the insistence of the eventual publisher, William Tinsley, after his acceptance letter of 5 May 1870. He asked Tom for a subsidy of £75 towards printing the first edition of 500 copies.

It was with a Hardyesque phrase that Tom ruminated on the implications of the eve of his thirtieth birthday:

'A sweet face is a page of sadness to a man over thirty.'

Time, he added, was producing 'the raw material of a corpse'.

On 16 May 1870, Hardy returned to Westbourne Park Villas - to work for Arthur Blomfield and also Raphael Brandon in Clement's Inn - though he retained the Cornish commission and returned there for a holiday with Emma in mid-August. He was back in Bockhampton a month later and as architect's clerk became the nation's latest anonymous author on 25 March 1871: 'Never will I forget the thrill that ran through me from head to foot when I held my first copy of *Desperate Remedies* in my hand.'

The Morning Post liked it, in a brief mention, but *The Spectator* spoilt Hardy's hopes, at great length. Better reviews followed - with everyone liking the cider-making scene - but they came too late. Returning from St Juliot on 3 June 1871, after spending his birthday with Emma, Hardy suffered the ignomy of seeing his first book remaindered for half a crown by W. H. Smith at Exeter Station.

Tom returned to other work for Crickmay and took lodgings at 1 West Parade, Weymouth. He designed schools in Radipole and Broadwey and the main cluster of villas around Greenhill at the northern end of Weymouth promenade. Bay windows and turrets came into vogue, as Belvedere-type watch-towers, so that the inhabitants could pretend to be mariners looking for their ships.

For Hardy, London called again in March 1872, and he lodged at 4 Celbridge Place, Westbourne Park. William Tinsley refunded him £60 from the sales of the book and

Hardy's mystery woman, his cousin Tryphena Sparks

Hardy acted as draughtsman for Professor Thomas Roger Smith of the Royal Institute of British Architects who had the contract for Board Schools in the capital. Hardy then sold the copyright of *Under the Greenwood Tree* to Tinsley for £40 and his second novel was in print by June 1872. He had found the title from his Chaucer:

'There will I make thee beds of roses
And a thousand fragrant possies,
A cap of flowers, and a kirtle
Embroider'd all over with leaves of myrtle.

'Under the greenwood tree
Who loves to lie with me
And turn his merry note
Unto the sweet bird's throat.'

This time the critics were less hostile. Tinsley was no prude, having published titillating speculation on Queen Victoria and her Balmoral gillie, John Brown. He asked Hardy to produce his 'new story' in instalments for *Tinsley's Magazine*. The novel *A Winning Tongue Had He* was accepted as a serial - starting in September 1872 - to be followed in book form by a first edition in three volumes, for £200. The title, however, was regarded as awkward.

In tribute to Emma it became *A Pair of Blue Eyes*. She stars as its short-lived heroine, vicar's daughter Elfride Swancourt, with Hardy himself being young architect Stephen Smith - 'pronounced moustache, and an incipient beard' - who comes to survey West Endelstow Church. Rival in love Henry Knight is a composite of reviewer Horace Moule and a prophetic Hardy imagining himself as a writer in later life. His eyes have 'lost their boy-time brightness by a dozen years of hard reading' and now 'permeated rather than penetrated'. Away went Knight's pen, 'beating up and down like a ship in a storm,' with just ten minutes to spare, in order to catch the late post.

The author had done just that in Cornwall, to correct the proofs for the first instalment, against a tight deadline in mid-August 1872. Thomas Hardy was no longer an architect.

Chapter Four
'Far From the Madding Crowd' to Marriage

PROOF THAT HARDY was winning admiration as an author came when one of Britain's leading editors, Leslie Stephen of the *Cornhill Magazine*, decided to poach William Tinsley's new writer. He wrote to Hardy with an offer he could not refuse:

'If you are, as I hope, writing anything more, I should be very glad to have the offer of it for our pages.'

Stephen followed this up with detailed advice on the plot for what we would call a soap-opera. While not demanding 'a murder in every number' it was 'necessary to catch the attention of readers by some distinct and well-arranged plot'. Tom realised the significance of the opportunity but for the time being he had to struggle at Bockhampton to finish *A Pair of Blue Eyes* for William Tinsley. Following it, he told Stephen, there would be a bucolic love story in which the principal love triangle would feature a lady farmer, her shepherd, and a cavalry sergeant. Hardy promised to submit it to Stephen.

Emma Lavinia Gifford, the first Mrs Thomas Hardy

Tom returned to London in June 1873 and visited Horace Moule in Queens' College, Cambridge. He returned to Bockhampton in July and the rest of the summer was spent writing *Far From the Madding Crowd*. The inspired title came from Grey's 'Elegy'. Hardy based Bathsheba Everdene and Gabriel Oak on Mrs Catherine Hawkins who, with bailiff Robert Spiller, farmed 525 acres around Waddon House at Portesham, with immense difficulty after the death of their shepherd, William Slade. Hardy apparently heard about them from his young cousin Tryphena Sparks who taught at the British School in nearby Coryates, in 1868, and with whom he is alleged to have had an affair.

The Puddletown of his youth, with his drunken wife-beating cousins, provided the basic setting and characters. Hardy's mother experienced dispossession and poverty in

Hardy visited Woodbury Hill Fair, Bere Regis, on a busy Sunday in September 1873

Melbury Osmond, where Aunt Martha had her fortune told, foretelling death in Canada. Her regimental husband in Hertfordshire - the prototype Francis Troy - and a tragic fourth man, bachelor farmer William Boldwood, completed the assemblage for the novel.

Hardy's fact-finding visit to Woodbury Hill Fair, crowded and joyful in a field enclosed by Iron Age earthworks above Bere Regis, coincided with the tragic death of his closest male friend and mentor, Horace Moule, in his rooms at Cambridge. The date, 21 September 1873, was a Sunday. Charles Moule had been summoned by telegram to come and comfort his brother. Horace was drunk and depressed, fearful that the self-destructive combination would cost him his job, and withdrawn to bed. As Charles sat reading in the next room he heard a trickling sound. On entering the bedroom he found that Horace had slit his throat with a razor. His last words were 'Easy to die' and 'Love to my mother'.

Hardy also felt the family's terrible hurt and shared their feelings of guilt and rejection for the rest of his life. The effect was a general sharpening of his character writing, initially blighting Boldwood in his current book, followed by a grim tide of misery and misfortune that overwhelms all the main male characters in his future work and climaxes in the life and loss of Jude Fawley. Hardy's work abounds in unlikely coincidences but he now knew from personal experience that fact is more chaotic than fiction.

The manuscript benefited from Stephen's interventionist style of editing, with improvements and insertions, which also acted as schooling for Tom in applied sophistication and technique. Judicious editing tightened the plot by deleting spurious conversations and observations. Stephen resisted Tom's tendency to incorporate lectures on self-improvement worthy of Samuel Smiles and his *Self-Help*. He assiduously removed off-putting descriptions of rural eating habits and took out pointless speculation about Sergeant Troy's apparent drowning. There was also a political bonus in that liberal changes made for neutral reading. Stephen's radicalism offset Hardy's conservatism.

The weakness of Leslie Stephen's editing style was that he tended to succumb to comments and letters of complaint about risqué sexuality. Stephen, a red-headed giant with a dog named Troy (purely coincidental), received corrected proofs from Tom at his Kensington home, 22 Hyde Park Gate, in December 1873 and it started to appear, anonymously, in the *Cornhill Magazine* for January 1874.

No one could question Stephen's place in the genetics of English literature. His first marriage was to Thackeray's younger daughter, Harriet Marion, and the second, to Julia Prinsep Duckworth, gave us Virginia Woolf.

Puddletown, the home of Hardy's cousins, provided the setting for Weatherbury village

Tudor Cottage, in banded stone and flint, with a 1573 datestone, was the Puddletown home of broadcaster Ralph Wightman

Tom went down to Cornwall to spend Christmas at St Juliot. He bought his copy of the *Cornhill Magazine* at Plymouth Station while returning to Dorchester on New Year's Eve. One surprise was that Stephen, always ahead of his time, had employed a female, Helen Paterson, as his illustrator. Another was that its reviewer in *The Spectator* identified another woman, George Eliot, as the author. Hardy failed to take that as a compliment and worried about becoming typecast as a yokel writer from rural roots. Class, or the lack of it, was an abiding obsession.

His own family were disappointed at the transparency of its content and setting, seeing the bucolic scenes as holding them up to ridicule.

They immediately realised that Casterbridge was the county town of Dorchester and Weatherbury the village of Puddletown. Discovering Hardy originals seldom requires much scholarship though he often moves the odd building or setting from one place to another or merges a couple of locations.

Weatherbury Upper Farm (Bathsheba Everdene's inheritance) is based on Waterston Manor in the Piddle meadows west of Puddletown. Its Great Barn is modelled on the monastic one at Abbotsbury. Little Weatherbury Farm (tenanted by William Boldwood) is Druce Farm, between Puddletown and Waterston. Nest Cottage (Gabriel Oak's home; since demolished) stood beside the bend on Chine Hill between Druce and Waterston. Yalbury Hill (where Troy and Bathsheba see Fanny Robin) is Yellowham Hill on the north side of the present A35, with the original course of the road being a hollow in the trees between the 1992-built embankment of the dual-carriageway and the other tarred road beyond it. The milestone on Mellstock Hill (which Fanny Robin reaches) is the columnar Roman milestone on Stinsford Hill, re-sited in 1988 in the landscaping on the south-west side of the roundabout. The Buck's Head at Roy Town (where Joseph Poorgrass stops for

The impressive south front of Waterston Manor, near Puddletown, which is inherited by Bathsheba Everdene in Far From the Madding Crowd.

Monastic thatch of the Great Barn at Abbotsbury which provides the setting for Bathsheba's barn (in both book and film) a mug of ale) was in Troytown hamlet, the name of which Hardy adopts for his 'wicked soldier-hero'. The 'little shop' close to Weatherbury church (passed by Bathsheba on an evening walk) was in the Palladian-style corner building in the Square at Puddletown. The gallery of the parish church, Weatherbury (where Gabriel is singing) appears as itself, being the intact 1635-dated gallery in St Mary's church, Puddletown. Weatherbury Vicarage (visited by Gabriel) was at Dawney House, which was the old vicarage at Puddletown.

Pummery Fair, as it was locally known, was held in Iron Age banks of Poundbury Camp on the outskirts of Dorchester. Casterbridge Barracks are the former Artillery Barracks in Poundbury Road, Dorchester, which are now the county's Territorial Army Headquarters. Casterbridge Grammar School (attended by Francis Troy) was founded by a Hardy forebear, one Thomas Hardye, in 1569, on a site adjoining the south side of Napper's Mite in South Street, Dorchester. Grey's Bridge (over the River Frome) appears under its own

The Roman milestone on Stinsford Hill before being moved clear of modern roadworks

Druce Farm featured as Little Weatherbury Farm, tenanted by bachelor farmer William Boldwood

41

The former 'little shop' on the corner of the Square in Puddletown

name on the London Road into Dorchester. A chestnut avenue (used by Fanny Robin to avoid Casterbridge) is Salisbury Walk on the almost flattened line of the Roman east wall of Dorchester. Casterbridge Union House (where Fanny is heading) is the Dorchester Union Poor Law Institution, known to all as the Workhouse, built in 1836 in Damer Road, Dorchester. The clock over South Street Almshouse (passed by Joseph Poorgrass on his way to the Workhouse) is that above Napper's Mite. The Corn Exchange (where Bathsheba faints in Boldwood's arms) appears as itself and is in North Square, Dorchester. Casterbridge Gaol (Boldwood in custody) is Dorchester Prison, also beside North Square. The White Horse Hotel, at the bottom of High East Street, appears as itself.

Further afield, Sherton Turnpike (where Gabriel catches up with Bathsheba) is West Hill Cottage, the turnpike cottage on the Longburton side of the junction of the A352 with the A3030, south of Sherborne. Budmouth Races (Troy loses more than £100) is Weymouth Race Course, which was on the edge of the marshlands at Lodmoor. Lulwind Cove (Troy fakes his drowning) is Lulworth Cove. Greenhill Fair (Troy disguised as Dick Turpin) is Woodbury Hill Fair at Bere Regis. Kingsbere (through which sheep are driven) is Bere Regis.

The Square at Puddletown in an Edwardian Raphael Tuck 'Oilette'

*New Street, Piddletown
(now Puddletown) in 1910*

*Daisies, dandelions and
cherry blossom complete the
Puddletown setting*

The King's Arms, Dorchester, into which farmer William Boldwood carries Bathsheba after she has fainted in the Corn Exchange

Tom was the first and only one of Jemima and Thomas's four children to marry.

No member of the Hardy family attended the ceremony at St Peter's church, Paddington. Neither did the bride's father, John Attersoll Gifford (1808-90), a former Bodmin solicitor, whose business failed through chronic alcoholism. The friction inside the Hardy family, and across the countryside around Dorchester, had been caused by their characterisations in *Far from the Madding Crowd*. John Gifford's objection to the liaison seems to have been class-based and financial. Since the death of his mother in 1860 he had become desperately short of money. Emma was marrying beneath her, as she herself came to believe.

At the time, however, it seems to have been a happy day, as recalled in *Some Recollections* in 1911:

'The day we were married was a perfect September day - 17th, 1874 - not brilliant sunshine, but wearing a soft, sunny luminousness; just as it should be.'

Emma's uncle, the Canon of Worcester Cathedral, Dr Edwin Gifford (1820-1905), conducted the service. He had been delivering the Warburtonian Lectures at Lincoln's Inn, which were published as *Voices of the Prophets*, and went on to be Archdeacon of London. As an aside to marriage matters, Hardy himself accepted that his books were unsuitable for some purposes, as he told Virginia Woolf:

'None of my books are fitted to be wedding presents.'

Emma had been staying with her younger brother, Walter Gifford, at 54 Chippenham Road, Westbourne Park. Tom and Emma headed south for their honeymoon, via Martin's Hotel in Queen's Road, Brighton, to Rouen and Paris, where they spent the rest of the month at the Hotel St Petersbourg in the Rue Caumartin. Emma's diary records that their visit to Notre Dame is followed by La Morgue, as if this is the most normal of holiday venues:

'Three bodies - middle one pink. Their clothes hanging above them. Not offensive but repulsive.'

Chapter Five
Swanage and 'The Hand of Ethelberta'

MR AND MRS THOMAS HARDY arrived back in 'Dirty London' on Thursday 1 October 1874. After a few days of house-hunting, from the Freeman's Arms in Wimbledon, they moved into lodgings on 6 October, at St David's Villa, Hook Road, Surbiton. The reviews of *Far From the Madding Crowd* were largely favourable with the exception of that from Henry James in *The Nation*, New York, who found the only believable characters were 'the sheep and the dogs'. This was more than counterbalanced by *The Times* noting, of the human participants, that at least they were 'all working people' rather than the 'idle lords and ladies' of many novels. Hardy, however, was less than happy to be regarded as a working-class author. He also anguished over the tendency for everyone to compare his country folk with those created by George Eliot.

The result, taking shape from December 1874 and bringing Hardy a £1,250 deal, was that *The Hand of Ethelberta* would enter different territory. The Hutton brothers from *The Spectator* came out with the trite but timely advice that each book should be 'better than the last'. Emma encouraged Tom to move on from the peasantry and their cows to Jane Austen's polite society.

Below-stairs details came from the real lives of members of the Hardy, Hand (or Hann) and Sparks families and Tom's flirtations with his cousins. The heroine, Miss Ethelberta Chickerel, takes her name from the village of Chickerell, near Weymouth. The good news, in January 1875, was that the first edition in book-form of *Far From the Madding Crowd* was virtually out-of-print. One thousand copies had been printed.

In February 1875 *The Spectator* revealed its authorship - not by George Eliot, and not even by a woman - though the misconception persisted. On 19 March 1875, Tom and Emma moved back to Paddington, to Newton Road, off Westbourne Grove. The following day,

Hardy met Prime Minister Benjamin Disraeli to lobby for new copyright laws

he shared Leslie Stephen's disappointment as Cambridge were thrashed in the University Boat Race, by some nine lengths. Stephen made Hardy his confidant. He asked him to witness his renouncement of Holy Orders which formally closed an earlier chapter of his life.

Hardy found London increasingly expensive both financially and in its demands in social terms on the time needed for writing to deadlines. Everyone wanted to meet the successful new author. He had already shaken hands with the Prime Minister, Benjamin Disraeli, having joined a deputation of writers to urge reform of the copyright laws.

Emma and Tom took a train from Waterloo to Bournemouth on Monday 12 July 1875. They stayed for three nights in a guest-house and then took the steamer to Swanage Pier on 15 July. It was St Swithin's Day 'and the rain came down like silken strings'. An 'invalid captain of smacks and ketches', William Masters and his wife provided lodgings in West End Cottage, off Seymer Road. Bushes overhanging the path featured in Hardy's posthumous collection of verse, *Winter Words*, in the poem entitled 'The Lodging House Fuchsias'. The coxswain of the first Swanage Lifeboat, *Charlotte Mary*, William Masters ('Captain Flower' as Hardy names him) provided gruesome details of the way that 'the sea undresses' shipwreck victims 'leaving them naked'. He also explained the

Swanage was still a stone port in 1875 when Hardy sketched the method of carting stone into the sea, to a lighter, which rowed it offshore to a London-bound ketch

movements of double-tides. On 7 September, Tom and Emma sailed around the Isle of Wight in the *Heather Bell* steamer (renamed by Hardy as the *Speedwell* in *The Hand of Ethelberta*), to see the 'spot where the *Royal George* went down' at Spithead. Emma tells us there were 'not so many masts as I expected'. They came back in the moonlight at high tide from Bournemouth to Swanage.

The return to Dorset enabled Tom, belatedly, to introduce Emma to his family. Tom and Emma set off from Swanage at seven o'clock, 'packed as close as sardines' with 15 fellow-travellers on Sommer's Van plus another six picked up on the road. They arrived at Corfe Castle at 10.30 for breakfast and then a picnic with Tom's sisters Mary and Katie. The date was chosen so that the author could take notes on the third excursion of the newly formed Dorset Natural History and Antiquarian Field Club. Led by John Clavel Mansel-Pleydell, they arrived 'in a file of shining carriages' and were met by Thomas Bond, the local

The replacement Swanage Pier (with its predecessor in the foreground) about to host the Waverley *paddle-steamer*

The scene in Swanage Bay, full of stone boats of varying types and sizes, painted by M. Croft in 1869 in a view south-eastwards to the stone quay and timber pier (right, centre) and Peveril Point beyond

In Hardy's time there was a fuchsia bush beside the porch at West End Cottage in Swanage

Wareham Quay and the town's ancient South Bridge into the Isle of Purbeck, as it was until the end of Hardy's life

historian, who delivered the lecture in the castle ruins. Hardy incorporated the details, at length, into the new book and has Ethelberta attending.

It is with *Ethelberta* that the geography of Hardy's Wessex takes on regional completeness. Anglebury is Wareham where the Red Lion Hotel appears as itself. Sandbourne is Bournemouth. Wyndway House is Upton House between Poole and Lytchett Minster. Flychett is Lytchett. Rookington Park is Hurn Court (home of the Earl of Malmesbury, now Heron Court School) beside the River Stour between Christchurch and West Parley. Arrowthorne Lodge is Minstead Lodge, near the Rufus Stone, in the New Forest.

Knollsea is Swanage (though it is Studland that has Knoll House Hotel and Little Sea). Hardy's Knollsea was 'a seaside village lying snug within two headlands as between a finger and thumb'. Old Harry Rock, the famous chalk stack between the two bays, appears as itself, as does Nine Barrow Down in the Purbeck Hills. Corfe Castle becomes Corvsgate Castle (Corfe Gate being the ancient name for the gap in the hills) with the

Capital and Counties Bank and Mermaid Hotel, High Street, Yeovil

Norman Churchill of Waddock Cross, between Affpuddle and Woodsford, typical of the war veterans from Waterloo to the Crimea whose stories inspired Hardy

Castle Inn being itself, in East Street. Enckworth Court is Encombe House (home of the Earl of Eldon). Havenpool is Poole. Melchester is Salisbury. Solentsea is Southsea. London, Southampton and the French towns and cities appear under their real names.

Emma also took up writing at Swanage and produced *The Maid on the Shore*. Then the couple move on. The final proofs of *Ethelberta* were sent from St Peter Street, Yeovil, in March 1876, for the book version sub-titled *A Comedy of Errors*, published in April by Smith, Elder and Company. It was an edition of 1,000 copies. One was inscribed to Emma ('E. L. Hardy from the Author') but she never opened it, as was proved by uncut pages, when it was sold at auction in 1938. 'Too much about servants in it,' Emma was quoted as saying.

Though illustrated for the *Cornhill Magazine* by George Louis Palmella du Maurier, and promising so much, *The Hand of Ethelberta* failed to match the popularity of *Far From the Madding Crowd*. Hardy wanted to change direction again and suggested to Leslie Stephen that he should commission 'some tragic poems' as the next project. This was about the last thing Stephen wanted and it marked a parting of the ways though they remained friends. In May 1876, Tom and Emma took temporary lodging near Oxford Circus, in central London, and spent June touring the Rhineland and Belgium, where they visited the Waterloo battlefield, and returned to England from Antwerp.

From March to June in 1876 the Hardys lodged with Miss Elizabeth Harris and her sister at 7 Peter Street, Yeovil. They were searching for a home of their own in a Dorset town, away from Dorchester, that had been reached by the railway.

Chapter Six
Sturminster Newton and 'The Return of the Native'

COWSLIP TIME WAS spent house hunting in the Blackmore Vale, followed by a holiday in Holland and on the Rhine, and then Tom and Emma moved into their first furnished home in July 1876. The northern half of Riverside Villas, Sturminster Newton, was rented from Robert Young (1811-1908) and his family who lived nearby at The Hive, a three-storey house looking out across the River Stour from the ridge on the western side of the town. Young, a friend of parson-poet William Barnes, called himself 'An Olde Dorset Songster' and published dialect verse under the pseudonym Rabin Hill.

Hardy celebrated the view in his poem 'Overlooking the River Stour' and then proceeded to obstruct it with the most Victorian of trees, monkey-puzzles, planting one in front of

Below left: Riverside Villas from the north-west showing the room (top left) in which The Return of the Native *was written*

Below: Hardy's pastoral view of the River Stour and Blackmore Vale from Riverside Villas

each of the two villas. These led to confusion as to in which half of the house the Hardys had lived, as the southern monkey-puzzle outlived the northern one, but Hardy himself settled the matter when he returned to Sturminster with the Hardy Players in June 1921. They were entertained on the northern lawn by Mr and Mrs William Ponting. Hardy pointed up to the first-floor front room of their home. In his own hand he captioned a photograph of the same northern villa:

'House in which* The Return of the Native *was written - 1877.'

The countryman had returned to Dorset but not to his native heath. The lush green 'Vale of Little Dairies' around 'Stur' (as the market town is known) form a landscape that is a world away from the heather and gorse moorland of 'Egdon Heath' which stretched almost unbroken across the entirety of south Dorset from the back wall of Hardy's birthplace to the marshlands of Poole Harbour. It formed a suitably prickly background to the interwoven marital relationships of the *Return* story which had been rejected by serial editor Leslie Stephen despite Hardy's acceptance of 'the irritating necessity of conforming to rules which in themselves have no virtue'. Stephen, for all his private radicalism, personified Puritan prudery in public. *Blackwood's Magazine* and George Bentley, for *Temple Bar* magazine, also rejected it.

Hardy's wine bill, paid by this £1 19s cheque to brewers Hall & Woodhouse, on 18 November 1876

Above left: Colber Bridge, built in 1841, downstream from the bridge which carried the Somerset and Dorset Railway across the Stour

Above: Sturminster Castle, actually a fortified manor house, where Hardy made a nostalgic return for a theatrical performance of his work in June 1921

One wonders how any publisher could fail to see the commercial potential of a powerfully sombre opening, one of the finest evocations of landscape ever written, which nearly half a century later inspired the composer Gustav Holst to produce his tone-poem *Egdon Heath*.

Hardy's fourth approach was to Mary Braddon, the wife of Irish publisher John Maxwell, who edited *Belgravia* magazine. She liked what she saw but would only pay £20 for each of the 12 instalments though George Smith of Smith, Elder agreed to publish the book version, in three volumes, with Henry Holt buying the American rights, to publish in New York a month later.

The Return of the Native is set in the 1840s. Egdon Heath is the western extremity of the heaths between the Frome and Piddle valleys, extending 6 miles, from Black Heath at Stinsford eastwards to Throop Heath at Affpuddle. Rainbarrow, one of a group of three Bronze Age burial mounds, features as 'the pole and axis of this heathery world'. It survives on Duddle Heath, Puddletown, but is now overgrown with trees behind a tangle of rhododendrons. Mistover Knap is Green Hill to the south of Puddletown Beacon. Alderworth is Briantspuddle. The Devil's Bellows is Culpepper's Dish. Throope Corner is nearby at Throop Clump and Rimsmoor Pond appears as itself.

Tower of Affpuddle parish church, the East Egdon setting for the wedding in The Return of the Native

The Quiet Woman Inn was the Red Lion at Winfrith Newburgh - a thatched hostelry before being replaced by a modern roadhouse - and the name survives as the Silent Woman at Coldharbour, near Wareham. The latter, however, used to be known as the Angel Inn. The quiet woman, traditionally Anne Bolyn, was rendered silent on losing her head. The contemporary Quiet Woman Inn, in actuality, was at Halstock.

Blooms-End, in the Frome meadows, is Bhompston Farm. Stickleford is Tincleton. East Egdon church, beside the River Piddle, is Affpuddle parish church. Shadwater is Woodsford and Shadwater Weir, on the River Frome, is at Woodsford and formerly had the 'ten huge hatches' described by Hardy.

As part of his researches, Hardy walked to Shroton Fair on 25 September 1876 and returned after dark across the Iron Age banks of Hambledon Hill, where he nearly got lost in the earthworks. Up the valley, Tom visited the Toad Fair at Bagber Bridge, between Sturminster and Lydlinch, where a quack-doctor named Buckman provided freshly-cut toad legs in little bags which were hung around the neck as a cure for scrofula. The shock effect of the twitching legs may have brought psychological benefits.

The Hardys also attended concerts in the assembly rooms at the Swan Hotel in Sturminster. 'She is the sweetest of singers,' Hardy wrote, describing a young woman from Keinton Mandeville in Somerset. He was also charmed by a bullfinch near Cutt Mill which trilled with 'a metallic sweetness piercing as a fife'. A man used to come most evenings from Sturminster to the rise beside Riverside Villas in order to watch the sunset. One winter afternoon 'the west was like some vast foundry where new worlds were being cast'.

Christmas 1876 was spent at Bockhampton though he never introduced Emma to the rougher elements of the family in Puddletown, and the cousins with whom he had been romantically involved. A reminder of his own exploits below stairs occurred one summer evening in 1877 after the Hardys' servant, Jane, returned from an excursion to Bournemouth with her boy friend. In the early hours, Tom spotted her emerging from the shed behind the house, with just a night-dress over her shoulders. The tall figure of a man loomed behind her.

Emma reacted furiously, running downstairs and ordering the girl to bed, but by the morning Jane had disappeared. She had not gone back home. Later it was found she had moved into her lover's home in Stalbridge. The next news was that she was pregnant.

Sturminster Newton was still a market town though this became a memory by the close of the twentieth century

Hardy noted the fact, laconically, in his diary:

'Yet never a sign of one is there for us.'

It does at least imply that Tom and Emma were still having a sexual relationship. Though the marriage was soon to come under strain, this turned out to be their 'happiest time'. Tom summed up the period, in verse, as 'The Sturminster Newton Idyll'.

Chapter Seven
Weymouth and Wimborne

TOM AND EMMA BEGAN to feel that Sturminster was professionally and socially out on a limb. Dorchester still seemed too close to home and at the same time far removed from influential contacts in the cosmopolitan melting-pots. *The Return of the Native* was appearing in the *New Monthly* in the United States but financial concerns made it imperative that new work was commissioned.

The Hardys took the plunge and decided to give London another chance. They moved into 172 Trinity Road, on the corner of Brodrick Road at Upper Tooting, on 22 March 1878. The Larches, it was called, at the end of three-storey Arundel Terrace, 'Beyond the Last Lamp' near Wandsworth Common. Here, in Hardy's words, their 'troubles began' with distance and coolness coming between them, exacerbated by incessant wind and rain and sharing a persistent cold. Despite a deteriorating relationship, however, they were still able to collaborate on preparing and copying manuscripts.

The publisher Revd Charles Kegan Paul (1828-1902), who had been vicar of Sturminster Marshall in Dorset until 1874, introduced Hardy to the Savile Club. Their social set included Walter Besant (novelist), George Bentley (editor), Robert Browning (poet), J. W. Comyns Carr (playwright), Sir Patrick Maccombaich Colquhoun (law writer and oarsman), Edmund Gosse (poet), William Dean Howells (American editor), Henry Irving (actor), Joseph Knight (drama critic), Charles Godfrey Leland (American poet), Frederick Locker (poet), Alexander Macmillan (publisher), Richard Monckton Milnes (1st Baron Houghton, poet and biographer), William Minto (editor), Edward Henry Palmer (Orientalist), Walter Herries Pollock (author), George Smith (publisher) and Alfred Tennyson (1st Baron Tennyson, poet).

In September 1878, back in Dorset to research *The Trumpet-Major* - a romance set in the

Napoleonic Wars - Hardy called on dialect poet William Barnes at Came Rectory and dined with Harrow assistant-master Reginald Bosworth Smith at Bingham's Melcombe House. London sources included the British Museum and pensioners at Chelsea Barracks. Back in Dorchester on 1 February 1879, Tom was met at the South Station by brother Henry and his horse, Bob, in the family's work-wagon.

In London, in December 1879, Hardy's writing clique founded the Rabelais Club, holding their inaugural dinner in the Tavistock Hotel at Tavistock Square. Professional jealously, combined with homophobia, came to the fore as they took childish pleasure at turning down Henry James's application for membership. Ironically, years later, he briefly joined Hardy as a holder of the Order of Merit, between New Year's Day 1916 and his death on 28 February that year.

The poet Matthew Arnold called on Hardy in February 1880 and left him with the thought that 'energy is genius'. Tom borrowed the phrase a couple of days later in a condolence letter to Handley Moule, on the death of his father, the 79-year-old vicar of Fordington, Revd Henry Moule. The 'Moule Memorial Coffee Tavern and Parochial Working Men's Club House' was opened in his memory. The vicar's elder son, also Henry, was the first curator of Dorset County Museum.

Mowing the meadow on Pentridge Farm, across the river from Hinton St Mary, where William Barnes was born in 1801

The Royal Hotel on the Esplanade, overlooking Weymouth sands

In *The Trumpet-Major*, Overcombe is Sutton Poyntz, though its mill is nearby Upwey Mill. It was in 'an old woman's cottage near Overcombe' that Hardy saw a caricature of Napoleon 'as a maimed French eagle' hanging on a wall. He has his character Robert Loveday producing it from his pocket. Budmouth is Weymouth and Gloucester Lodge, where King George III stayed on his annual visits from 1789 till 1805, appears as itself. It is now the Gloucester Hotel. Budmouth Barracks is the Red Barracks, above Hope Square, which is now Wellington Court. On the slopes around Bincombe the 'Grand Old Duke of York marched his men to the top of the hill, and marched them down again'. Oxwell is Poxwell. Springham is Warmwell.

Leslie Stephen was the first to reject *The Trumpet-Major*. There is an anecdote to the effect that Stephen told Hardy: 'Heroines don't end up marrying the wrong men.' Hardy replied that in life they did so all the time. 'Yes,' was Stephen's riposte, 'but not in magazines!'

The string of rejections also included *Macmillan's Magazine* and Blackwood's *Edinburgh Magazine*. Then came a lunch at the Savile with Revd Dr Donald Macleod (1831-1911), the editor of *Good Words*, which lived up to its title with a commendation from the Society for Purity in Literature. Hardy was by now resigned, as he put it later, to moderating his prose 'in order to keep base life afloat'. The effect of Macleod's editing on Hardy's work was on the level of turning 'swearing' into 'profane noises' and making sure that dubious behaviour occurred on weekdays rather than Sundays.

Bathing machines on Weymouth beach as Hardy knew it, with the royal arms having been carried by the one in the foreground

The next literary project was *The Laodicean*. Named for the infamous people of Laodicea in the Book of Revelation, it broke the Dorset rustic mould, and was therefore set around the more neutral landscape of Dunster Castle and Taunton in Somerset. Combining the erotic and intellectual it brought an offer of £100 per submission for a year's monthly instalments. These appeared in the new European edition of *Harper's Magazine* with George du Maurier as illustrator.

Emma and Tom went away in August 1880 for their summer holiday in Le Havre and Normandy. Hardy went alone to Weymouth and then Bockhampton in mid-September. In October both Emma and Tom visited three of the Moule brothers in Cambridge. Horace's suicide continued to prey on his mind and Hardy claimed to have seen Wordsworth's ghost. He was also disturbed to see the candles guttering into 'most fantastic shapes' which the superstitious country folk in his own family would have seen as foretelling a death. Hardy took this personally and expressed concern that he had made inadequate financial provision for Emma.

Much of that winter was spent in Tooting in bed. Tom blamed his illness on an infection caught while swimming at Etretat. It seems more serious than that, with a haemorrhage causing him to pass blood, and then a stone from his bladder. For a time he feared the candles were right and he was dying. 'What a time I had of it,' he recalled.

Hardy, aged forty, in 1880

Emma not only nursed him but took dictation, for several months, to keep *A Laodicean* on schedule. Hardy was haunted by the recurrent dream of a multi-headed monster 'whose body had four million heads and eight million eyes'. He also blamed his poor health on the London's damp and stagnant air and agreed with Emma that they had to return to Dorset as soon as possible.

Wimborne, their chosen place, was the county's major railway junction with lines radiating five ways, to Dorchester, Bath, Salisbury, Southampton and Poole. The final chapter from the capital, with Hardy able to use the pencil again, completed *A Laodicean* in April 1881.

On 25 June 1881, they spent their first night at Llanherne in The Avenue at Wimborne. It was an almost Biblical experience. Released from London's murky sky, into the clear country air, Emma and Tom stood in the conservatory, thrilled by a clear view of Tebbutt's Comet. Hardy realised that the unexpected mystery object in the sky would be regarded at Bockhampton and Puddletown as an ill omen but for the new intellectual elite

Above & below right: *Wimborne Station, opened in 1847 and closed in 1964, was Dorset's closest connection to the capital during Hardy's time in the town*

Below: *The line towards Wimborne, from West Moors level crossing*

astronomy was widening natural horizons. Tebbutt's course was calculated with awesome confidence. No one on Earth is going to see it again until the fourth millennium. This sets Hardy thinking about his next novel where he writes:

'That the magnificent comet of 1881 would not return again for thirty centuries had been quite a permanent regret for him.'

'Lanhern' is the current spelling for the brick-built detached house which has become No. 16 Avenue Road. When the Hardys moved in, The Avenue was a gravel carriageway, and land towards Grove Road was a pasture. Hardy befriended land agent Robert Douglas whose brother was the Scottish author and landowner Sir George Douglas. Emma liked Sir George who encouraged them to holiday in Scotland. They visited Edinburgh and Loch Lomond in August 1881 and stayed with Sir George at Springwood Park, Kelso, in September 1891.

Llanherne, No. 16 Avenue Road in suburban Wimborne, with a blue plaque to commemorate Hardy's residence

Tom particularly enjoyed the company of retired county court judge Henry Tindal Atkinson whose daughter played for them on the piano at their family home, Berghmote. A younger friend, George Pike, lived in Grove Road from 1877 to 1894. George Lock was their hairdresser in the High Street. Hardy also befriended his physician, Dr George Batterbury, and allowed the town's Shakespearean Society to meet at Llanherne. Local architect Walter John Fletcher accompanied Hardy on country walks. Fletcher designed St John's church, consecrated in 1876, to cater for the new residential district between Rowlands and Wimborne Station. The Society for the Protection of Ancient Buildings asked Tom to keep it informed on any threats to Wimborne Minster. Hardy at Wimborne was as integrated into local society as he would ever be. Unlike Dorchester life, town gossip here was no threat, lacking problems of past associations and overlapping lives.

London and international publishers maintained their interest in Tom. Short stories, such as *Destiny and a Blue Coat* and *Five Weeks in the Life of an Heiress*, appeared in the New *Quarterly Magazine* and *Harper's Weekly*. *The Thieves Who Couldn't Help Sneezing* was published in a Christmas annual for children. Robert Buchanan commissioned *The Impulsive Lady of Croome Castle* for his weekly magazine *Light*. Then Thomas Bailey Aldrich (1836-1907) signed him up for the *Atlantic Monthly*, to produce the much more substantial *Two on a Tower*, which Hardy began sketching out in November 1881. This was to be a scientific romance. Hardy wrote to the Astronomer Royal, to arrange a visit to Greenwich Observatory, on the pretext that he was considering fitting out a West Country

Wimborne Minster, hosting a performance of the musical Otter for Common Ground, *has been at the heart of Dorset culture since Saxon times*

Hardy kept an eye on restoration work at Wimborne Minster for the Society for the Protection of Ancient Buildings

tower to house a telescope. Writing began in earnest in the New Year. The procedure was 'lamentably hurried' and there was no time for proofs. Emma helped with the copying.

Then came a theatrical diversion. The dramatist J. W. Comyns Carr collaborated with Hardy in producing a stage version of *Far From the Madding Crowd* which ran at the Prince of Wales Theatre, Liverpool, from 27 February 1882, for a fortnight. It was then booked to go to Bradford. The production starred Miss Marion Terry as Bathsheba Everdene and Charles Kelly as Sergeant Frank Troy. Hardy visited Comyns Carr at 26 Oxford Street, Liverpool, and attended the last performance in the city on Saturday 11 March. In order to streamline the plot, the playwright had dropped Farmer Boldwood and substituted gypsy Will Robin, as the avenging character. Overspill audiences resulted from what the *Liverpool Daily Post* described as the 'theatrical scandal' it generated in the London newspapers.

In December 1882, the orbit of Venus, goddess of love, put the planet directly between Earth and the Sun, in a rare line-up not to be repeated until 2008. Eclipses had a particular appeal to Tom who was fascinated by the immensity of inter-stellar space. Through 'Adonis-astronomer' and rector's son Swithin St Cleeve of *Two on a Tower*, he proves to be abreast of new knowledge - incorporating Harvard astronomer Edward Charles Pickering's work on variable stars - at a time when the universe was thought to comprise our one galaxy, whereas we are now told there are upwards of one hundred billion of them. All that between two transits of Venus!

Hardy realised the competitive nature of scientific discovery:

'Publish it at once, in some paper, and nail your name to it, or somebody will seize the idea and appropriate it - forestall you in some way.'

He also writes of sending off information in triplicate which was precisely what he was doing himself with two copies of each chapter being posted to America - in case one was lost at sea - and the other destined for the book publisher in London. The conclusion to *Two on a Tower* is told in two arrestingly short sentences:

'Viviette was dead. The Bishop was avenged.'

Hardy's horizons were spreading again. Emma and Tom escaped from the writing, 'playing truant' in Paris in October 1882, and on their return came to the conclusion that

For the location of Two on a Tower, *Hardy chose this monument in Charborough Park*

Right: *For the setting for* Two on a Tower, *Hardy placed it in the wood around this obelisk at Weatherbury Castle, Milborne St Andrew*

Far right: *For the architecture of* Two on a Tower, *Hardy selected the memorial to Admiral Sir Samuel Hood in Butleigh Wood above Compton Dundon, Somerset.*

as with Tooting, Wimborne was too close to its river. They tried to acquire building land from the Ilchester Estate on Stinsford Hill, between Dorchester and Hardy's home village though without success. The short story *The Three Strangers* for *Longman's Magazine* in London and *Harper's Magazine* in Boston was followed by *The Romantic Adventures of a Milkmaid* in *The Graphic*.

Wimborne and its countryside is woven into *Two on a Tower* with Warborne as the Minster town. Welland House is Charborough House. As for the setting, its observatory tower is moved to Rings-Hill which is Wetherbury Castle hill-fort, at Milborne St Andrew. Rings-Hill Speer, a Tuscan column, is also imported into the story. In actuality it is the Hood Monument between Compton Dundon and Butleigh in Somerset. Welland village is the hamlet of Almer near Sturminster Marshall. This makes the perfect example of a three-tier Hardy location. *Our Exploits at West Poley* was a boys' adventure story sub-titled *A Tale of the Mendips.*

There was also time at Wimborne to respond to a long-standing request for a 15,000-word factual article on 'The Dorsetshire Labourer' for *Longman's Magazine.* Published in July 1883, it made no mention of the most famous of them - the six Tolpuddle Martyrs.

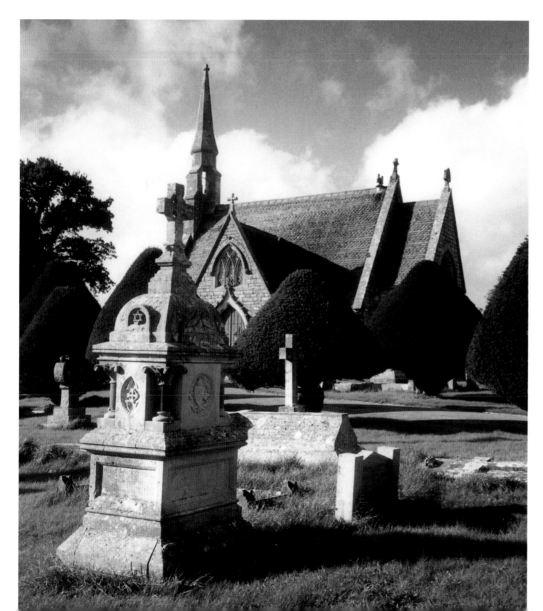

Victorian mortuary chapel and monuments in Wimborne cemetery

Wimborne in miniature at the Model Town

Chapter Eight
Max Gate and 'The Mayor'

THE FIRST HOME IN Dorchester for Tom and Emma, at 7 Shire Hall Lane, has since been demolished for a forensic laboratory with the name incorporated into Glyde Path Road. They moved in during June 1883 and stayed for two years. Hardy visited William Barnes at Came Rectory and walked with him to Winterborne Came parish church beside Came House. The author had reverted to being an architect and was drawing the plans for a villa on the two-acre plot he had bought from the Duchy of Cornwall on the north side of the Wareham Road, opposite the former turnpike toll house known as Mack's Gate which is under the course of the present A352. Max Gate was chosen as the name for their new home. To the east, below tree-covered Conquer Barrow and the ploughed-out bank of Mount Pleasant henge monument, is an 1835-dated marker stone: 'M B of the B of D' (Municipal Boundary of the Borough of Dorchester).

The land cost £450 and the builders, the family firm of Hardy and Son, are said to have received a total of £1,000. Income was also increasing, with £600 being offered by *Macmillan's Magazine* for *The Woodlanders* in twelve parts, which he based around his mother's memories and countryside. Newspaper files were scoured for key moments and incidents for a story set around the county town which was to be titled *The Mayor of Casterbridge*. He started on this in this in April 1884 and was also working on *Interlopers at The Knap* and *A Tryst at an Ancient Earthwork*.

Meanwhile the chalky ground at Max Gate was providing Hardy with his own collection of Roman-British antiquities. Clearance of the site took place in November 1883. Trenches for the foundations disturbed three burials in elliptical graves, cut into the bed-rock, with skeletons crouched in womb-like poses rather than being laid out. One had a bronze brooch at its head which probably fastened a shroud. Six black-ware pottery vessels were in a variety of tribal Durotrigic or imitation Roman shapes of the 1st century AD. There

Hardy called on dialect poet William Barnes at Came Rectory, near Dorchester

Came Rectory, near Dorchester, where Hardy visited dialect poet William Barnes

Right: *Creation of the Dorset County Museum was supported by Hardy*

Far right: *Dorchester's Roman defences, comprising a great earthen bank, at Colliton Walk above The Grove*

was also a splendid 22.5 centimetre high cream-coloured ring-neck flask that had been made at the Corfe Mullen kilns at the time of Claudius, the emperor who undertook the AD 43 invasion of Britain.

More skeletons were found later. From the forehead of one Hardy took a pair of penannular-shaped brooches which had been joined by another early Roman fibula of the Maiden Castle class. Nearby there was a pit with the burnt bones of a horse and an iron spearhead. Covering one of the skeletons was a large sarsen stone. Hardy had this 'set up at Max Gate as a menhir' in a newly-planted hedge.

Hardy's menhir in the hedge still puzzles Max Gate visitors

Later finds, from the flower beds and vegetable garden, included decorated potsherds of top-class imported Samian ware from later in the first century. Hardy quite rightly cherished his private collection of conquest-period native and Roman pottery and other finds. They were kept in his private study, the contents of which went to Dorset County Museum, in 1936. Excavations at Colliton Park, behind Wollaston House and below

Hardy died before relics of 'old Rome' arose from Colliton Park, Dorchester

C. S. Pridaeux and Sebastian Evans excavating Maumbury Rings, Dorchester, in 1913

Above: Replica Armada-period fire-bucket and the almost levelled Roman Wall (left) *beside Salisbury Field, Dorchester*

Below: Roman floor in the Town House, Dorchester, with toga-togged Chris Copson explaining its underfloor heating system

Archaeologist Chris Copson with the Waitrose mural of the prehistoric sacred site that lay below its underground car park

Poundbury Camp, have since gone some way to justify Hardy's claim that one can sense old Rome throughout the streets of the town. Howard Pell, in 1973, spent a couple of days showing me hundreds of third-century Christian graves cut into the chalk that was being exposed by building work on the north-west side of the town. In all they must numbered upwards of 2,000.

Then Chris Copson found remarkable evidence of earlier sacred monuments, built on an Avebury-like scale, during excavations before construction of the A35 bypass between the Trumpet Major public house and Hardy's garden wall at Max Gate. Their site is now an incongruous cutting which does nothing to enhance the literary setting as it cuts off the Hardy connections from the town. Similar prehistoric earthworks are depicted on a tiled mural beside the lifts to the Waitrose supermarket in Dorchester. Red circles on the floor of its underground car-park show the site of holes for posts and stones. They confirm the prior significance of a town that is no Chester, Colchester or York but firmly belongs in the middle rank of Roman provincial centres.

Above left: *Section of Roman Wall at Top o' Town, Dorchester, given to the town by Lucia Catharine Stone in 1886*

Above: *Victorian plaque set in brickwork above the Roman Wall*

West Dorset MP Oliver Letwin and folk singer Billy Bragg were among those appearing as Romans on the Dorchester hustings for the general election at the end of the next millennium. Hardy would have been delighted that 'old Rome' was back in town, if only for a day, beside a villa-sized Roman Town House in the shadow of County Hall. As a result of his influence, Lucia Catharine Stone preserved a 'fragment of Roman Wall' at Top o' Town, and presented it to 'the Mayor and Corporation of Dorchester' on New Year's Day in 1886.

Tom Hardy took his brother, Henry, on holiday to the Channel Islands in August 1884. In 1885 the author found a wealthy new admirer in Lady Eveline Alicia Juliana Herbert, daughter of the 3rd Earl of Carvarnon, who married the 5th Earl of Portsmouth. Between them the two families owned 102,000 acres, including estates in Devon and Somerset, and might well have seduced the Hardys into moving westwards, were it not for the fact that the Max Gate project now anchored Tom firmly in Dorchester.

They moved into the new house on 29 June 1885. Hardy was far from happy, recording:

'. . . a fit of depression, as if enveloped by a leaden cloud'.

Roman mosaic and stone coffin as Victorian centrepiece to Dorset County Museum

Max Gate, south-east turret and conservatory from the front lawn

Below: *Drawing room and its view of the front lawn*

Below right: *The stairway*

The local surgeon, Frederic Bazley Fisher, attended to a recurrence of his Tooting bladder problem but with only partial success. Friend and poet Edmund Gosse and Robert Louis Stevenson, a national celebrity since publication of *Treasure Island* in 1883, were among the first visitors to Max Gate.

Mrs RLS, seldom lost for words, found Hardy to be 'a pale, gentle, frightened little man'. As for Emma, 'ugly is no word for it!' They called in August 1885 when RLS was living in Bournemouth and being treated for chronic tuberculosis. He was in the process of completing *Kidnapped* and *Dr Jekyll and Mr Hyde*. Thinking a change of air would ease his suffering, and choosing Dartmoor for the purpose, he stopped off en route for a few days at the King's Arms, High East Street, Dorchester. In the event, taken ill again, he never progressed beyond Exeter.

'He came out to my house unexpectedly,' Hardy recalled:

'He appeared in a velveteen jacket with one arm in a sling. He particularly wanted to see the room I wrote in, but as I had come into the house quite recently, I had not settled into any definitive writing place.'

Family life featured the first of a series of cats, Kiddleywinkempoops-Trot, and Moss was Hardy's Labrador bitch. Their regular walk was a mile eastwards to Stafford House which is now the home of *Gosford Park* scriptwriter Julian Fellowes and wife Emma Kitchener.

Extended visits were made to Max Gate by Lilian and Gordon Gifford, the children of Emma's brother Walter. Dorset's other well known writer, parson William Barnes who was as old as the century, died on 7 October 1886 and Hardy wrote his obituary for the Athenaeum. He also gathered £400 in subscriptions for what took life-size form as the bronze statue by Roscoe Mullins, unveiled beside St Peter's church in High West Street in February 1889.

Set-back from the corner of Alington Avenue and Syward Road, Max Gate is an austere three-storey Victorian villa, much like those Hardy designed for Greenhill at Weymouth, with rather squashed lines and a token turret. It was given its initial privacy by a brick wall, followed by a screen of hundreds of Austrian pines, behind which Hardy withdrew though he accepted appointment as a Justice of the Peace. Both his sisters, Mary and Kate, were also back in the county town, teaching at the National School for Girls in Bell Street.

Robert Louis Stevenson, in August 1885, was one of the first visitors to Max Gate

Above: *Shire Hall and its plaque (top) to the Tolpuddle Martyrs who were convicted here in 1834*

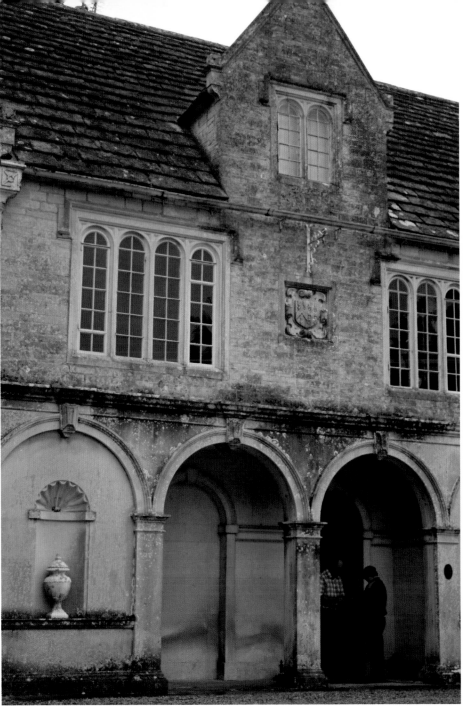

Stafford House, alias Froom Everard House

Responding to criticism and playing to his strengths, in *The Mayor of Casterbridge*, Hardy created a strong and plausible combination of characters and plot. Leading participant Michael Henchard represented an amalgam of the powerful Henning and Trenchard family names from Wolfeton Manor at Charminster. All the events and misfortunes, including wife-selling and a 'skimmity-ride' to shame moral outcasts, had their source in the files of *The Dorset County Chronicle*, which are preserved today in the library of Dorset County Museum. Robert Louis Stevenson was impressed and asked in May 1886 if he might dramatise the novel. Hardy accepted the offer but nothing materialised.

Few of the Dorchester locations are difficult to identify. The Antelope Hotel and King's Arms appear as themselves, as does the Three Mariners hostelry further down the north side of High East Street. The latter was an Elizabethan building, since replaced by a Victorian public house, and now redeveloped. High Place Hall is Colliton House in the grounds of which County Hall was built in the 1930s. Barclays Bank, on the east side of South Street, has a blue plaque proclaiming itself as Michael Henchard's home. Court House is Shire Hall in High West Street. The Market House is the Corn Exchange in North Square. The adjoining Town Hall is itself, built in 1792, though replaced by the present Town Hall in 1848. Priory Mill is the former Friary Mill. The High Street is High West

Barclays Bank in South Street, Dorchester, with a plaque recording its place in fiction

High West Street from Top o' Town, Dorchester, in 1853

*Genteel Fordington,
around St George's church*

*Corn Exchange and turret,
designed by Benjamin Ferrey
in 1847, replaced the building
Hardy described*

Street. Corn Street is South Street and Cornhill. Back Street is Trinity Street. North-West Avenue is The Grove. Chalk Walk is Colliton Walk. Bowling Walk is Bowling Alley Walk. West Walk is West Walks. Durnover is Fordington. Mixen Lane is Mill Street there and Peter's Finger the King's Head, Mill Street, Fordington.

The Ring is Maumbury Rings, the Roman amphitheatre, at the junction of Maumbury Road with Weymouth Road. Ten Hatches Weir, is itself, though only five of the hatches survive on the River Frome upstream from Grey's Bridge. Mai Dun is Maiden Castle hill-fort. Cuckoo Lane is itself, between the main road and Higher Bockhampton.

Whereas Casterbridge is Hardy's home town setting, the Hintocks of *The Woodlanders* is based around the delightful landscape of his mother's upbringing. Composite vignettes feature the woods on either side of Bubb Down Hill and High Stoy on the mixed soils between the Dorset Downs and the western edge of the Blackmore Vale. Great Hintock amalgamates his mother's home at Melbury Osmond and Minterne Magna where Hardy's elder sister started her teaching career. Little Hintock brings together settings at Stockwood and Hermitage. Hintock House is up on the downs, based on Turnworth House at Turnworth - where Hardy rebuilt the parish church - with Oakbury Fitzpiers being the village of Okeford Fitzpaine in the vale to the north. The story coincides with divorce reform legislation in 1858. Fred Pitfield, in *Hardy's Wessex Locations*, explains that the topographical mixture may have come about to protect both the author and inhabitants from the risqué nature of the plot running counter to Victorian morals:

Fordington High Street, towards the artisan quarter of the county town

'Hardy, in an attempt to avoid any possible allusions to real people, seems deliberately to have made some of the locations difficult to identify precisely - even some of the fictional characters encounter difficulty in finding Little Hintock.'

Marshcombe is Middlemarsh and Revellers' Inn the former Revels Inn at Lower Revels Farm, Buckland Newton, which was notorious for cudgel fighting on the outcome of which large sums were bet. This village appears as Newland Buckton. Tutcombe is

Above left: *High Street, Fordington, drawn by S. L. Grassby*

Above right: *Fordington-based threshing machines transformed Dorset's agriculture*

Traction engine on hire from Eddison & de Mattos Ltd at Dorchester

Above left: Entrance and top-row views of the Roman amphitheatre at Maumbury Rings

Above: Ten Hatches on the River Frome, upstream from Grey's Bridge

Multiple Iron Age ramparts, engineered for slingstone warfare, on the southern side of Maiden Castle

Above: *Bubb Down Hill, from old man's beard in a hedge by the railway, at the heart of the Hintocks*

Above right: *Melbury Bubb comprises a church, house and farm*

Lewcombe and Delborough is East Chelborough. The Earl of Wessex Hotel at Sherton Abbas is the former Digby Hotel in Digby Road which was rebuilt to coincide with the arrival of the railway line from Salisbury and London in 1860. It now accommodates The Digby dormitories of Sherborne School. Sheep Street in Sherborne is Cheap Street (with the latter deriving its name from the mediaeval word for a market).

Church Farm, with the church beside it, on the north side of Bubb Down at Stockwood

The Woodlanders was finished on 4 February 1887, with Hardy noting down 8.20 pm as the moment of achievement:

'Thought I should feel glad, but I do not particularly - though relieved.'

The following month, when the volume appeared, he took Emma on holiday to Italy. While Hardy picked violets on John Keats's grave in Rome, *The Woodlanders* brought him a new offer, of £1,000 from Tillotson and Son in Bolton for the serial rights to the next full-length novel. That would be *Tess of the d'Urbervilles*. Such was the reaction to *The Woodlanders* that Edmund Gosse was sent out to scour London for a copy one Sunday in 1887. Robert Louis Stevenson wanted to take it on his final journey from England to America. From there he would continue to the Pacific, Sydney, and death in Samoa in 1894.

Hallowe'en pumpkin on the wall (left) *beside Manor Farm at Stockwood*

Chapter Nine
On to 'Tess' and 'Jude'

THE SUMMER OF 1887 saw the celebrations for Queen Victoria's golden jubilee with Tom and Emma joining in at the Savile Club. Hardy the social animal, amid lords, ladies and the literati, declared himself 'neither Tory or Radical' but 'an intrinsicalist'. In January 1888 he hit upon the idea of effectively copyrighting his Dorset-based Wessex - telling Sampson Low to call their cheap reprints of his titles 'the Wessex Novels' - pointing out that he was the first to use it in fiction 'and it would be a pity to lose the right to it for want of asserting it'.

'The Withered Arm' headed a new two-volume collection of short stories published by Macmillan in the spring. Other successful minor works, occasional articles, and royalties from popular reprints paid the living expenses at Max Gate, provided a holiday in Paris in May 1888, and rented lodgings at 5 Upper Phillimore Place, Kensington. Once again, London brought illness, variously described as 'one of the worst cold in the heads' and a 'rheumatic attack'. Ideas for the next two monumental works pre-occupied Hardy's thoughts. These coalesced around the names of the new characters. The forename Angel, for Tess's husband, comes from Angel Grey on a family memorial in the north aisle of Stinsford Church. Jude can also be found in a church, on a brass plaque at Frome St Quintin where Hardy's Swetman ancestors lived. The story of *Tess* took shape over the winter of 1887-88 and was developed in tandem with that of *Jude*.

Much of the background for *Tess* came from family anecdotes, many incorporated in detail, and in Jude the thwarted aspirations of Hardy himself are combined with the abiding memory of the horrific suicide of his close friend Horace Moule. Among miscellaneous Moule family documents in my collection there is the following unattributed and undated pencil note:

'Eldest son Henry, Curator of the Museum. Clare family in **Tess of the d'Urbervilles** *is Moule family. Horace like Angel Clare. He was the most powerful influence on Thomas Hardy. Horace was the pivot of Traphine's tragedy. She was 40 years his junior. Horace eight years older than Thomas. In his early novels the heroes were architects. [In] 1870 Hardy met Miss Gifford and for two years from July '70 Hardy was estranged from Horace and Traphine. There's never a villain in Hardy, only victims.'*

Tess, who Hardy admitted was based on a real person, came from close to home. His paternal grandmother, Mary Head from Fawley, Berkshire, remembered precisely what she was doing when she was told of the guillotining of Marie Antoinette - ironing, with the pattern of the gown being etched on her mind - which must be a universal reaction to such shocks through the ages, from demise of King Harold at Hastings and the execution of King Charles to the deaths of President Kennedy and Princess Diana. Hardy's grandmother had been a close companion to tragedy, with her father dying shortly before she was born on 30 October 1782, and her mother following in the spring of 1788.

Mary Head was seduced as a teenager, by John Reed, and gave birth to an illegitimate daughter, Georgiana Reed in 1796. A few months later she was committed to the House of Correction in Reading on a theft charge. An unlucky few in such a predicament found themselves hanged, and many more were transported to Australia, but her accusers spared her by failing to present their evidence in court on 25 April 1797. The age as given in the records is two years less than Mary's, but as Robert Gittings has pointed out, such errors are not unusual for orphans and her presence in the Bridewell would explain how she came to hear shrieks 'under the lash' as documented in a Hardy poem. Mary Head left for domestic service in Dorset and was working locally when she became pregnant by Hardy's grandfather and married him in Puddletown on 19 December 1799.

Tess as a name, of which Hardy would have been aware, was that of the Royal Navy frigate which guarded Napoleon in exile on St Helena. She once lost eight seamen, working in the rigging, in a lightning strike. Under the command of the novelist Captain Frederick Marryat, HMS *Tess* fought in the first Burmah War, in 1825, and went on to have a religious after-life, beginning on 17 May 1927, as a floating Mission to Seamen. That was in George's Dock, Liverpool. Stripped and fitting with pews she sufficient space for the regular attendance of 800 sailors. William Scoresby was the chaplain.

The working title for *Tess*, half finished in September 1889, was *Too Late Beloved*. At this stage there was no d'Urberville ancestry to link 'succulent' Tess Woodrow and 'handsome horsey dandy' Alec Hawneferne. Publisher William Tillotson was dismayed that the story of a seduced maiden would outrage his readers and cancelled the contract. Hardy, now reasonably secure financially and no longer prepared to re-write to suit market forces, offered the manuscript to Edward Arnold of *Murray's Magazine*. He also felt that ladies should be able to go through life without being made aware of the tragedies brought about by 'immoral situations'. It went next to Mowbray Morris of *Macmillan's Magazine* who similarly recoiled from the sexuality and thought that Tess was not merely seduced but was portrayed as making herself available for seduction.

Hardy was now forced to bend in the face of continuing prudish pressure and it is a bowdlerisation serial that eventually appeared. Hardy's triumph was to return to these chapters and restore, and reassemble for the book that followed, the story of the epic heroine of English literature. Delay had brought benefits, and the transformation of Tess Woodrow into Tess Durbeyfield brought to her misfortunes the poignancy of lost inheritance, plus an implied incestuous irony to new abuses.

No wonder editors and clergymen regarded Hardy as a scandalously subversive writer who was exposing the hypocrisy behind Victorian values. *Tess of the d'Urbervilles*, whatever the opinion leaders might think, was *A Pure Woman* according to Hardy's sub-title for the work. Hers was a 'real existence' not only in the sense of having had living sources but for consolidating Hardy's personal position by bringing fame and fortune. He had produced an everlasting best-seller which instantly propelled him into top society. The inevitable criticism included a description of the characters as 'stagey and farcical' in the *Saturday Review* which found it 'an unpleasant story told in a very unpleasant way'. Others showered it with rapturous acclaim. To both admirers and detractors it became a book that it was fashionable to read and discuss.

The settings for *Tess* cover the whole of Dorset. The background is the riches to rags real life tale of the Turberville family whose former manor house at Bere Regis is now Court Green pasture opposite the Royal Oak Inn. Their other mansion, Woolbridge Manor beside the River Frome, survives but became absorbed into the Weld family's Lulworth Castle Estate. Land around Bere Regis went to the Drax family of Charborough Park. In Bere village the West Street hostelry is now the Drax Arms but the Turberville name predominates inside St John the Baptist parish church. There is a Turberville window, with stained glass featuring the arms of families connected by marriage, and a cluster of

Tess Cottage at Marnhull

Turberville tombs and brasses. Below, in the south aisle, the floor slab of the Turberville vault records:

'The Door of the Sepulchre of the Ancient Family of the Turbervilles.'

The story begins in Marlott, which is Marnhull, where Tess Cottage on Walton Elm Hill was known as Barton Cottage. It is now Tess Cottage. Rolliver's alehouse is probably the former Lamb Inn, now Old Lamb House, at Walton Elm Cross (rather than the Blackmoor Vale Inn in the village). The Pure Drop Inn is definitely the Crown Inn. Other locations in the Valley of the Little Dairies - the Blackmore Vale - include Stourcastle for Sturminster Newton and Nuttlebury for Hazelbury Bryan where the Antelope Inn appears as itself. Above the vale, Shaston is the real-life name for Shaftesbury, being its contraction on turnpike milestones. Bulbarrow, Nettlecombe Tout and Hambledon Hill appear as themselves on the chalk escarpments. Owlscombe is Batcombe and the Cross-in-Hand, a Roman column used as a boundary marker on Batcombe Hill, is the Cross and Hand. A shepherd warns Tess:

The parish church of St John the Baptist at Bere Regis

The Tuberville window in the parish church at Bere Regis

Medieval Turberville tomb in Purbeck marble at Bere Regis

'Tis a thing of ill-omen, Miss.'

Flintcombe Ash is Plush, a downland hamlet, above Piddletrenthide. Stagfoot Lane is Hartfoot Lane at Lower Ansty where Lane Inn is the old Fox Inn, on the corner with Cothayes Drove, rather than the present Fox Inn at former Ansty Brewery. Trantridge is Pentridge, near Chaseborough, which is Cranborne. There the Flower-de-Luce hostelry is the Fleur-de-Lis.

Westwards, Evershead is Evershot where Benvill Lane is almost itself (Benville Lane) and the Sow-and-Acorn is the Acorn Inn. The village also has its Tess Cottage. Emminster is Beaminster. Long Ash Lane is itself, now the A37, on the upland section of the Roman road between Dorchester and Ilchester. Crimmercrock Lane, taking itself name from an ancient burial chamber, was Cromlech Crock Road and is now the A356 across Toller Down. Both roads are near Chalk-Newton which is Maiden Newton. Abbot's-Cernel is Cerne Abbas.

Nuttlebury is Hazelbury Bryan

The Cross and Hand on Batcombe Down – ''Tis a thing of ill-omen,' Tess is told

The Antelope Inn at Hazelbury Bryan

In the Valley of the Great Dairies - beside the River Frome eastwards from Dorchester - Talbothayes Dairy is Lower Lewell Farm, east of West Stafford, which appears as Lew Everard. Wellbridge is Wool and Wellbridge Manor is Woolbridge Manor. Kingsbere is Bere Regis and Green Hill is Woodbury Hill which was famous for its agricultural fair. Sandbourne is Bournemouth. Bramshurst Court is now Moyles Court School, near Ringwood. Stonehenge appears as itself as does Wintoncester, almost, as Winton is from its Latin name and the signature of the Bishop of Winchester.

Tess as the ultimate Hardy heroine has her male equivalent in Jude. Hardy had his originals in memories of Horace Moule from Fordington Vicarage and Hardy's Puddletown uncle, cobbler John Antell. The latter, self-taught in the classics, also succumbed to black moods and alcohol abuse, deteriorating into a violent drunkard. The companion of *Jude the Obscure*, taking shape in 1890, is Susan Florence Mary Bridehead. The Florence came from Florence Henniker, married daughter of Lord Houghton, Viceroy of Ireland. She was the subject of one of Hardy's unconsummated flirtations. Susan Mary Jeune was a mutual friend at Arlington Manor, Berkshire, where much of the story is set. Aspects of Sue Bridehead's character, Hardy admitted, were 'suggested by the death of a woman' in 1890. This may have been his closest cousin, teacher Mrs Tryphena Gale - nee Sparks - at Topsham, Devon, on 11 May. John Antell's widow also died in 1890.

Hardy took the decision to shave off his beard in March 1892 - though retaining a wide moustache - before sitting for his portrait by William Strang. He heard that his father, crippled with rheumatism, had taken to his bed on 27 April. Thomas Hardy senior held out until 20 July 1892 and was commemorated by a poem 'On One Who Lived and Died Where He Was Born'. Mary was returning to Bockhampton from laying flowers on the grave on 17 September 1892, when Tom and Emma passed in a carriage, just as Stinsford House burst into flames and 'the firelight now flickered' across the churchyard. On going back to London, on 12 October 1892 Hardy attended the funeral of the poet laureate, Alfred Lord Tennyson, in Westminster Abbey but found it 'less penetrating than a plain country interment'.

Tom was currently writing the serial version of *The Well-Beloved*. Set on the Isle of Slingers, as Hardy named Portland - which was his 'Gibraltar of Wessex' - it features Jocelyn Pierston searching for female perfection across three generations of the same family. There is a 20-year gap between the episodes in which he desires Avice Caro, then her daughter Ann Avice, and finally grand-daughter Avice. Needless to say, this being a Hardy plot, each affair is destined to fail before marriage. These unattainable visions

Then-and-now glimpses of Flintcombe Ash which is the hamlet of Plush in a downland valley near Piddletrenthide

Tess Cottage at Evershot, on the corner of Back Lane above the churchyard, retains its rustic look

Lion Gate, guarding the entrance to Melbury Park, at Evershot

paralleled Hardy's personal quest for his ideal Tess. She appeared before him for the rest of his life. He saw Tess in a succession of dairymaids, shop assistants, stage actresses and travellers on the train, as he admitted to Virginia Woolf in later life:

'I used to see people now and then with a look of her.'

Hardy stayed at Aldeburgh with Edward Clodd over Whitsun in 1894. Fellow guest Grant Allen summed up the weekend with a couplet:

'How late we tarried, slow and tardy. Yet loth to lose one tale from Hardy.'

It was as *Hearts Insurgent* that Jude's story appeared in Harper's *New Monthly*, in 1895, and captured younger readers for Hardy's work, including 29-year-old H. G. Wells. Another was Agnes Grove, married daughter of General Augustus Pitt-Rivers, who danced with Hardy in the Larmer Tree Grounds on 4 September. 'For Agnes' was his

The Royal Oak at Cerne Abbas, a Hardy favourite, providing a pit-stop for riders

Lew Everard is West Stafford

poem in her honour. A vivacious and 'voteless' globe-trotter she was a thoroughly modern woman. Michael Pitt-Rivers told me that his grandmother once entered the drawing room at Rushmore House and found Agnes 'sprawled stark naked across the chaise-longue'. Agnes told her:

'You are now looking at the body of the most beautiful woman in the world.'

Tess was still winning hearts, being dramatised by Johnston Forbes-Robinson for the London stage, and promised to leading lady Mrs Patrick Campbell. The earlier novels, reprinted during the decade by Osgood, were also moving with the times. Revisions included explicit language with the heroine in *The Woodlanders* now being able to say: 'He's had you.' *Jude the Obscure* was written without Emma having her usual moderating influence and was going to offend her Protestant fundamentalism.

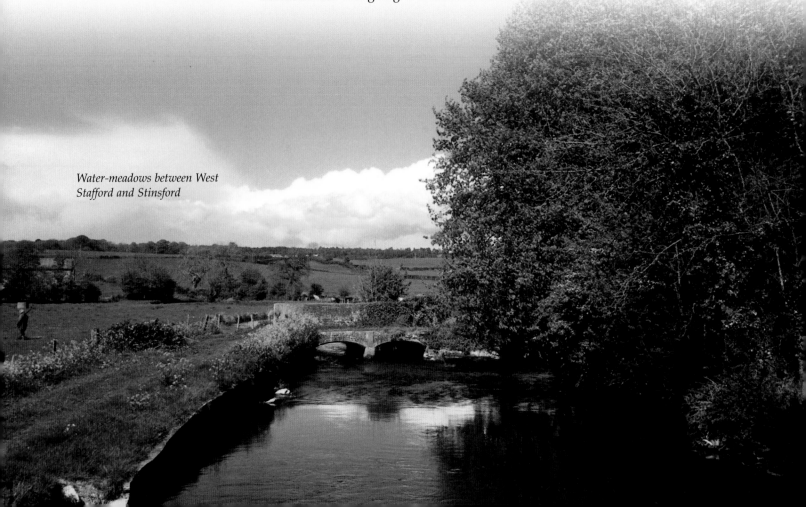

Water-meadows between West Stafford and Stinsford

Left: Lewell Mill, on the River Frome, at West Stafford

Below: The Wise Man Inn at West Stafford

Above: *Jacobean Woolbridge Manor at Wool is the pivotal place in Tess's tragedy*

Left: Medieval Wool Bridge, over the River Frome, beside Woolbridge Manor (right)

Milking time near Hardy's home in a Walter Pouncy photograph

Georgian transportation threat, on Wool Bridge, with a 1668 date-stone

Hay-making in the Frome meadows, photographed by Walter Pouncy

The reviewers, sadly, were more in tune with Emma Hardy than the avant-garde Agnes Grove. 'Jude the Obscene' the *Pall Mall Gazette* railed, denouncing 'dirt, drivel, and damnation'. *The World* in New York went for 'Hardy the Degenerate'. Even his friend Edmund Gosse described it as the most 'indecent' work of fiction he had ever read. 'Garbage' was the epithet of the Bishop of Wakefield who claimed to have consigned it to the hearth. 'Filth and defilement' said Wesleyan missionary Thomas Gunn Selby. To G. K. Chesterton, Hardy was:

'. . . a sort of village atheist, brooding and blaspheming over the village idiot'.

Months later, changing his club to the Athenaeum, Hardy still felt the opprobrium. On the other hand, *Jude* was proving a decisive commercial success, selling 20,000 copies over the winter of 1895-96. J. M. Barrie set the novels into context by making a comparison with the popular writings of Richard Jefferies and concluding that Hardy:

'. . . 'knows the common as well as Mr Jefferies knew it; but he knows the inhabitants, as well as the common'.

Hardy shaved off his beard and sat for his portrait, by William Strang, in 1892

Portland appears as the Isle of Slingers in The Well-Beloved, *named for the ancient slingstone pebbles of the Chesil Beach* (centre)

Castletown Pier and Portland Harbour which was constructed over a period of several decades during Hardy's lifetime

Above: *Romantic ruins on Portland's eastern cliffs, with Rufus Castle overlooking the site of medieval St Andrew's church*

Right: *Portland juts out into the English Channel with the Pulpit Rock being Dorset's southern extremity*

Far right: *Verne Citadel fortress, cut off from the island by a great chasm, is now Portland Prison*

Despite Hardy's rheumatism and Emma's shingles they set off with bicycles (his black 'Rover Cob' and her blue 'Grasshopper') for Dover and peddled across Flanders in October 1896. The book version of *The Well-Beloved* rounded off the output of major novels. Completed in December 1896, after painstaking tinkering with the beginning and end, it closed the second phase of his working life. On 2 March 1897, *Tess* stepped from the page and appeared abroad, rewritten for the New York stage by Lorimer Stoddard and played by the director's wife, Mrs Minnie Maddern Fiske.

Hardy joined the madding crowd for educational entertainment provided in Larmer Tree Grounds by General Augustus Pitt-Rivers, and became an admirer of the latter's daughter Agnes

Tess, Hardy's epic heroine, as she was portrayed in a Victorian print

Chapter Ten
Hardy the Poet

HAVING ACHIEVED financial security, with the reassurance of a lifetime of royalties that would continue to enjoy copyright protection for a further half century, Hardy could at last write what he wanted. That was poetry. It had been his personal predilection for years, since he pondered over advice from Coventry Patmore that this was the 'proper form of expression', but magazine editors would only pay well for serialised novels which were the soap operas of their day. Poetry, even in its Victorian heyday, was eclectic and esoteric, free to venture beyond conventional barriers to thought provided it did so in code. Hardy realised the poetic irony of the medium:

'If Galileo had said it in verse that the world moved, the Inquisition might have let him alone.'

Dorset's highest hill, Pilsdon Pen, rises to 908 feet, with the most western of the big hill-forts dominating the Marshwood Vale

On the other hand, if Hardy had anywhere further to take the English novel it would see him crucified by reviewers and churchmen, branded as a pornographer and turned with Emma as well into a social pariah. Thomas Hardy the novelist was about to re-invent himself as Thomas Hardy the poet.

His first great topographical poem, from 1896, is 'Wessex Heights'. As well as Bulbarrow Hill and Pilsdon Pen in Dorset it features Inkpen Beacon above Newbury and Wills Neck overlooking the Vale of Taunton Deane from the Quantock Hills. Hardy wrote in a letter at the time:

Athelhampton Hall, Dorset's finest Tudor mansion, features in both the novels and poems

'Wessex Heights will always wring my heart, for I know when it was written, a little while after the publication of Jude, when he was so cruelly treated.'

The poem's four peaks each represent a woman in Hardy's life. Easy to identify are his mother, Jemima Hardy, and wife, Emma. The enigmatic third 'ghost in Froom-side Vale, thinned-lipped and vague in a shroud of white' has been linked by Professor J. O. Bailey to cousin Tryphena Sparks, in *The Poetry of Thomas Hardy*. Bailey confidently identifies the fourth woman as the Honourable Mrs Florence Henniker (who lived until 1923):

'As for one rare fair woman, I am now but a thought of hers,
I enter her mind and another thought succeeds me that she prefers;
Yet my love for her in its fullness she herself even did not know;
Well, time cures hearts of tenderness, and now I can let her go.'

In 1897, after visiting Queen Victoria's diamond jubilee event by day-trip from Basingstoke, Tom took Emma to Lausanne and Zermatt, in the shadow of the Matterhorn. They then visited Salisbury, in August 1897, whilst building work was being carried out at Max Gate. Emma and Tom attended evensong in the cathedral a couple of times, as he recalled in *The Life*, to be quoted a century later by ex-Prime Minister Edward Heath::

'Upon the whole, the Close of Salisbury, under the full summer moon on a windless midnight, is as beautiful a scene as any I know in England - or for that matter of that elsewhere.'

He wrote the following day to his sister Kate - 'My dear Katherine' - to mitigate her own bad memories of Anglican teacher training in the King's House ('emptied for the holidays so you would have no unpleasant reminders') and added a natural history observation:

'Bats were flying around the gates of the Bishop's Palace.'

The magic moment was also enshrined in his poem 'A Cathedral Façade at Midnight'.

On returning to Dorset, Tom took Rudyard Kipling on a cycling holiday, in order to persuade the nation's other great poet to retire to the county. In the event, Kipling chose Sussex, where Bateman's is his National Trust shrine. Hardy's cycling distances expanded in 1898 when he accompanied brother Henry on a visit to a cousin in Bristol. Major-General the Honourable Arthur Henniker-Major, husband of novelist Florence Henniker who features in Hardy's poems, called at Max Gate while on manoeuvres with Southern Command.

Wessex Poems, which appeared in the autumn, was Hardy's first collection of verse. It included many love poems based on 'little fancies' but only a single one to Emma who was understandably offended.

'I can scarcely think that love proper and enduring is in the nature of men,' Emma wrote to Miss Elspeth Thomson who married *The Wind in the Willows* author Kenneth Grahame. She cautioned that 'at fifty, a man's feelings too often take a new course altogether' and then makes it clear that she is writing from personal experience:

'Eastern ideas of matrimony secretly pervade his thoughts, and he wearies of the most perfect and suitable wife chosen in earlier life. Of course he gets over it usually somehow, or hides it, or is lucky!'

Emma concedes there may be the occasional happy marriage but thinks these are restricted to Christians 'if both are' - with the word 'both' underscored - making it clear that Emma is the Christian and Thomas a non-believer. She may not have entirely given up hope as she presented him with a new Bible as his birthday present in 1899. They were in London and Hardy went to Buckinghamshire to hear one of his leading ladies, in social terms, reciting Thomas Gray's 'Elegy' beside the poet's grave at Stoke Poges. She was the stunningly attractive Helena Zimmerman, fiancee of the Duke of Manchester, and the words had particular poignancy for Hardy as they had given him his first really successful book title:

'Far from the madding crowd's ignoble strife ...'

A journey from Salisbury to Newbury, in October 1899, was memorable as Tom's first trip in an automobile. He still preferred a bicycle, he told Edward Clodd:

'. . . though going at great speed on a highway was a novelty.'

Tom and Emma were brought together by their pets, sharing the grief when Moss died after being beaten by a tramp, and were active members of the Anti-Vivisection Society. Hardy urged that there should be an international convention outlawing the use of horses in cavalry assaults and restricting their part in warfare to transporting soldiers and supplies. Emma was an effective polemicist with frequent and strongly worded letters to the press such as that in *The Daily Chronicle* of 8 September 1899 on the behaviour of Britons abroad who 'trailed our national reputation in the dirt' by attending a bull-fight

Above and left: *Sad Sedgemoor: the site of the last major battle on English soil, in July 1685, where the Duke of Monmouth's rebel army came to grief in Bussex Rhyne, having its echoes in Hardy's poetry*

Portrait of Thomas Hardy the poet

in Boulogne. American literary critic William Lyon Phelps visited Max Gate in the summer of 1900 and found Hardy catering for a herd of cats from all over Dorchester. The resident ones were Markie, Snowdive, Pixie and Comfy.

The Hardys joined the English liberal backlash against the war in South Africa, making Thomas the new century's first war poet, and giving Emma a political platform, to point out that 'the Boers fight for homes and liberties - we fight for the Transvaal Funds, diamonds and gold'. Hardy also felt sympathy for the British fighters, cycling to Southampton and back - a total distance of 100 miles - to wave goodbye to Dorset boys as they went up the gang-plank into a troopship. His powerful poem 'The Dead Drummer' - later re-titled 'Drummer Hodge' - remained the best of its kind until a new generation wrote from first-hand experience on the Western Front. In 'The Souls of the Slain' the ghosts fly home from South Africa like migrating moths.

Emma weathered a storm of personal problems. She nursed her widowed sister, Helen, who was terminally ill with dementia in Lee-on-Solent, while her niece, Lilian Gifford, looked after Tom at home. Nephew Gordon Gifford, also living at Max Gate, was sent out into the world to follow Hardy's first career and became an architect for London County Council. Helen died on 6 December 1900 and personified 'By the Century's Death-Bed' which we know as 'The Darkling Thrush'. Bertha Newcombe, a friend of both Emma and Tom, described Emma's plight in a letter to Ellen Gosse:

'It is pathetic to see how she is struggling against her woes. She . . . is a great bore, but . . . so kind and good hearted, and one cannot help realising what she must have been to her husband.'

Poems of the Past and Present did well with its first edition selling out but initial and subsequent sales - only 500 copies had been printed - were only a fraction of those of the novels. Hardy was now primarily a poet but to his public he remained a novelist.

London's literary Whitefriars Club visited Max Gate in May 1901 to pay homage. War continued to stir his mind but it had to be the conflict he heard about in his childhood. An epic poetic drama would be safely rooted in the Napoleonic Wars of a century earlier.

Hardy's mother, Jemima, died aged 90 at Higher Bockhampton on Easter Sunday in 1904. The date was 3 April and she was buried at Stinsford a week later. The family group at the funeral was headed by sons Tom and Henry and daughters Mary and Kate. Hardy at

63-years-old had a shrinking physical presence with H. G. Wells and others expressing surprise that he was such a 'grey little man'.

Like his mother he suffered from rheumatoid arthritis and increasing deafness though in later life publisher Newman Flower said he enjoyed telephone conversations with those who phoned Dorchester 43:

'He grew to love the telephone with the allegiance of a boy to his first big bag of marbles.'

That familiarity and freedom took many years to evolve. Hardy originally insisted that callers left messages and would not use the apparatus. Only after a friend demanded to speak to him personally did he begin to relent. The biographer Arthur Christopher Benson attempted a primitive form of telephone conferencing, when he tried to host a discussion between himself, Henry James and Thomas Hardy. It failed when neither could hear him or each other. On the other hand it would be exaggerated to claim that either of the Hardys was reclusive, as was proved on 1 September 1905, when Emma hosted a garden party at Max Gate for 200 members of the Institute of Journalists.

Portrait of Thomas Hardy, Order of Merit, in his Max Gate garden

Hardy's working life was being rounded off by an intellectual triumph which received almost all his attention between 1902 and 1907. This was what Hardy pronounced as 'The Dinnasts'. It passed muster. Adventure writer Arthur Quiller-Couch was by no means alone in seeing in *The Dynasts* 'the grandest poetic structure planned and raised in England in our time'.

Perhaps the strongest critic was his wife who not only placed Bibles in the guest rooms of Max Gate but opened the pages for the recommended reading of the day. They would then be told by her husband that the 'local cult called Christianity' would not outlast the 'systems of the Sun'.

Chapter Eleven
Second wife Florence

THE MYSTIC WRITER Edward Clodd (1840-1930), a wealthy merchant banker with the London Joint-Stock Bank Limited from 1862 till 1915, lived at Aldeburgh on the Suffolk coast. Precisely the same age as Hardy, he must have wondered quite what was going through his old friend's mind in 1909 when he pleaded that a 'young friend and assistant' whom Clodd had been inveigled into taking out to dinner and the opera - for reasons to be explained - was now 'so very delicate' that she needed regular holidays at the seaside.

The lady, less than half their age, was Florence Emily Dugdale (1879-1937), a teacher from Ealing, who was a struggling creative writer. Her lucky break seems to have come about in June 1907 when Hardy gave her a signed copy of his *Wessex Poems*. She was soon having her work edited and extended in Hardy's distinctive plodding style.

Florence had a 'kind friend' in Dublin, the surgeon Sir Thornley Stoker (1845-1912), who gave her a typewriter. Three of his four brothers were active in London's intellectual society - namely the author Bram Stoker, Thomas Stoker who was the retired Chief Secretary of India's North-Western Province, and George Stoker who was principal physician at the London Throat Hospital. Canon Edward Brooks told me over lunch in Fordington Vicarage in 1968 that he heard from an elderly parishioner that she had mentioned to Florence her abiding interest in how wives came to meet their husbands. Florence told her:

'I was introduced to mine by Dracula!'

She became Hardy's regular companion in London but Emma was kept in ignorance. Emma lived a separate life at Max Gate, behind the dormer windows of an attic boudoir, which was her 'sweet refuge and solace'. She went off alone to Calais for the autumn of

Old Pump Court, St James Street, Shaftesbury, in 1903

1908. Having 'developed a mild form of religious mania', Emma progressed into harmful eccentricities that were a constant cause of distress to Tom. She joked with Edmund Gosse that she beat her husband each morning 'but only with a rolled-up copy of *The Times*'.

Hardy was offered a knighthood by Prime Minister Asquith but turned it down, fearing the social implications of the semi-detached couple being reunited as Sir Thomas and Lady Hardy.

Tom lamented the removal of the music gallery in which his family had played in St Michael's church at Stinsford. In 1909 he suggested that if an organ was required 'the old west gallery should be re-erected'. That was achieved in 1996.

Most outside contacts were now through the mail though that was now at its most efficient. Their new post-box, in the front wall beside Alington Avenue, was a red Edward VII box 'No. 107, Max Gate' for 'Letters Only'. Its hours of collection, Monday through to Saturday, were '(1) 7.30 am (2) 12 noon and (3) 6.15 pm'. Sunday collection was at 4.40 pm.

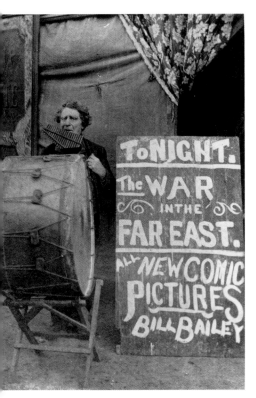

Early cinema in Dorset for the Japanese-Russian war of 1904

Tom managed to carry off a potentially tragic farce worthy of one of his own novels. He was guest of honour at Covent Garden Opera House for composer Baron Frederic d'Erlanger's Italian production of *Tess*. Its first production, in San Carlo Theatre, Naples, on 10 April 1906 had also been more dramatic than expected. Mount Vesuvius began to erupt that evening. At the London premiere, on 14 July 1909, Queen Alexandra sat in the royal box for what the *Manchester Guardian* described as 'one of the largest and most brilliant [events] of the season'.

Hardy invited both his wife and his mistress. Tom attended to Emma and Florence was taken in hand by Edward Clodd. Emma knew Clodd but disliked him for having renounced Christianity. Tom slipped off to see Florence at the intervals. To *The Daily Telegraph* the production was 'a success bordering on a triumph that it richly deserved'.

In August 1909, Tom and Florence went on holiday together to Aldeburgh, Suffolk, followed by Ventnor in the Isle of Wight in March 1910. They then made annual return visits to Aldeburgh.

Hardy eventually engineered a meeting between Emma and Florence, at the Lyceum Club, Piccadilly, in 1910 which went so well that Florence was invited to Max Gate. It was a very twentieth-century relationship, revolving around Florence's flat near Baker Street, in which 70-year-old Hardy introduced Florence as his 'secretary-help' and researcher.

On 6 May 1910 the nation grieved when King Edward VII died of heart failure and was succeeded by his son, the Duke of York, as George V. For Hardy it turned into a significant personal milestone as one of the new King's first decisions, in his personal gift, was to appoint Thomas to the Order of Merit. The offer to join its elite ranks came in a letter from the Prime Minister on 2 July, with the ceremony arranged for the 19th, but Emma was unable to share the honour as she had returned to Dorset in poor health. Tom, Emma and Florence had their public moment together later in the year with the presentation of the freedom of the borough of Dorchester. They were accompanied by the poet Henry Newbolt.

Christmas 1910 was a happy one for Florence who was now secure in her position as heir-apparent.

Hardy published a series of macabre short stories in the *Fortnightly Review*, as *Satires of Circumstance* in 1911, and a similar piece on *Blue Kimmy: The Horse Stealer* - hanged at Ilchester Gaol on 25 April 1827 - which he passed off in the *Cornhill Magazine* as the work of 'F. E. Dugdale'. Emma asked Florence to type her manuscript of *The Maid on the Shore* - which was at least in her own words - but time was not on her side. Suffering chronic pain with gall-stones, Emma employed 14-year-old Dolly Gale from Piddlehinton as her personal masseur, and she only descended the three flights of stairs for dinner. The domestic staff noted that Tom and Emma no longer spoke. Emma's only weekly outing was in a bath-chair, pushed by the gardener, to the Sunday morning service at St George's, Fordington. She took her poems, in a collection called *Alleys*, and a manic collection of apocalyptic religious effusions entitled *Spaces*, to the printers in Dorchester.

Thomas Hardy's postbox in the Max Gate wall

To mark Hardy's 71st birthday, on 2 June 1911, Henry Newbolt and W. B. Yeats visited Max Gate to present the gold medal of the Royal Society of Literature. Emma recovered enough to host the garden party and made a couple of visits to the sea at Osmington Mills and theatre at Weymouth. The respite was temporary and Emma was terrified of surgery.

An international tragedy intervened, with the *Titanic* disaster, and Hardy responded with a poem - 'The Convergence of the Twain' - published in the Memorial Programme on 14 May 1912. Emma was in agony when American admirer Rebekah Owen visited Max Gate and in an even worse state when Dolly Gale went upstairs to the boudoir at 8 o'clock on the evening of 28 November 1912. A few days earlier there had been a 'violent row' when

*Hardy and Florence Dugdale,
his second wife, contemplating
the future on the beach at
Aldeburgh*

Emma made one of her rare visits to Hardy's room and 'saw the table littered with the remains of food'. They had hardly spoken since but now she was crying out for Tom. He hesitated in his reactions and by the time he had finished shuffling his papers and climbed to the attic she could no longer respond to him. 'Em, Em, don't you know me!' he said. Within five minutes she was dead.

Dr Benjamin William Gowring signed the death certificate, with impacted gall-stones and a stomach ulcer being the cause, and Hardy sent a telegram to Florence. Emma's earlier *Recollections* survive but after the funeral Hardy discovered two other large manuscripts in her room. One was entitled *The Pleasures of Heaven and the Pains of Hell*. The other was *What I Think of My Husband*. Hardy read enough of them to realise the tragedy and implications of the contents. He sat in front of the fire into the night, slowly peeling off the pages, one by one, and consigned them to the flames. Florence described them as 'those diabolical diaries' in a letter of March 1913.

By Christmas Florence Dugdale was in residence, dismissing housekeeper Florence Griffin, and also ousting Emma's niece, Lilian Gifford, who made the last of her regular visits. Hardy was remorseful with guilt in a long bereavement for Emma that spilled over into 'an expiation' of words, in a sequence of more than fifty poems during the next two years, expressing a passion he had denied to her in life. It was described by Newman Flower as a process of 'self-castigation'.

The world continued to shower honours on Hardy. Cambridge University bestowed an honorary literature doctorate and fellowship of Magdalene College. Mary Hardy realised that her brother would have on his mind the memory of Horace Moule and his suicide there four decades before:

'This is to congratulate you on the honour Cambridge has now conferred on you. It seems as if it came from that dear soul, whose dust, for so many years has been lying in Fordington churchyard.'

In *A Changed Man*, Hardy featured Horace's father, Revd Henry Moule - Fordington's vicar for more than half a century - who was regarded as the saviour of his people for having publicly held Prince Albert and the Crown-owned Duchy of Cornwall to account for neglect of their duties as landlord which had exacerbated Dorchester's cholera epidemic in the middle of the nineteenth century. With the loss of more old friends and childhood loves, Hardy was paying his respects in verse to a growing army of ghosts.

Chapter Eleven
The Wizard of Wessex

FLORENCE EMILY DUGDALE became the second Mrs Hardy in Enfield parish church, Middlesex, at eight o'clock in the morning of 10 February 1914, with the chosen hour 'being in keeping with the retiring disposition of the well-known author'. Only the priest and three others were present. Florence's father, headmaster of the nearby elementary school, gave away his daughter. The witnesses were Florence's sister Marjorie and Tom's brother Henry.

A wedding breakfast followed after which Florence and Tom took the train for Dorset just minutes before the press were alerted and 26 reporters headed for the Dugdale family home at 5 River Front, Enfield. Hardy issued a statement carrying the myth that Florence had been Emma's friend. Even close friends like Edmund Gosse were surprised that they had never been introduced to the literary woman who was 'my long-time secretary'. In penance for the white lies he made a trip to Cornwall in May to visit the Gifford tombs, but Henry Hardy felt too unwell for accompany him, and Florence reluctantly took his place:

'The whole process was melancholy.'

Worse was to come with 'such a sad, sad, book' of poems about Emma. Hardy anguished in a letter to Florence Henniker, on 17 July 1914, about these verses that:

'. . . I wrote just after Emma died, when I looked back at her as she had originally been, and when I felt miserable lest I had not treated her considerately in her latter life. However I shall publish them as the only amends I can make.'

The saving grace, bringing Hardy his greatest pleasure of these final years, was bought by Florence just months before the outbreak of the Great War. This was a Caesar terrier named Wessex. The two became inseparable and such was Hardy's tolerance and laxness that he delighted in seeing the creature molest his guests, including the surgeon Sir Frederick Treves, and allowed it to eat from the table. Cynthia Asquith found herself having to 'contest' every fork-full and something similar happened when the Hardys called on Lord and Lady Ilchester at Melbury House. Dinner had to be shared.

As well as making sure the postman came no further than the gate, he famously took a bite out of author John Galsworthy, and howled uncontrollably one evening in the presence of William Watkins, a Welshman, who founded the Society of Dorset Men in London. Hardy and Watkins searched the Max Gate grounds for an intruder. There was none, Newman Flower tells us, but for Hardy it was confirmation of what he had long believed. Wessex had mysterious powers and rightly sensed that something was wrong:

'Watkins left Max Gate at ten o'clock, returned to his hotel, and died two hours later in his sleep.'

Winston Churchill sending off the Royal Naval Division, to Gallipoli, in the rain at Blandford in 1915

Remembering the war, at Colehill, in 1921

Hardy was 'long obsessed by the incident' and joked to visitors who complained of feeling unwell that he could reassure them with some confidence that they were 'not yet in immediate need of Dr Gowring'. It was unknown for Hardy to laugh but he could chuckle as 'a happy smile would flick across his face like a flash of summer lightning'. Life revolved around Wessex and his eventual fate became Florence's abiding nightmare. She feared 'the inevitable Wessex tragedy' in which the truculent creature was either run over by a car or seized by a policeman and put down before she could intervene and win a reprieve.

The primary medium of the new century was film. The first of Hardy's novels to make the transformation was *Tess*, through a deal with Louis Vincent, in 1911. A year later the project passed to 38-year-old motion picture producer Adolph Zukor who founded the Famous Players Film Company. He arranged for cottage exteriors to be filmed in that far-flung part of Wessex known as New England, in the United States of America, in 1913.

Hardy made a day trip by train for the trade showing of *Tess* at Pykes Cinematograph Theatre, Cambridge Circus, London, on 21 October 1913. His reaction is unknown but according to Dorchester auctioneer and amateur actor H. A. Martin the film was 'grotesque' though his substantive critique centred on 'its interminable herd of cows'. Here he could invoke his professional knowledge:

'Even now, and much less frequently in the period of the novel, dairies of cows seldom exceed 80.'

How quickly times change. The next cinematographic offering was to have been *Far From the Madding Crowd*, by portrait artist and film-maker Sir Hubert von Herkomer (1849-1914). He bought the rights for £150 but died before production could start. Hardy immediately struck a new deal with American producer Larry Trimble and actress Florence Turner in 1915. Together they owned the Turner Film Company which had studios at Walton-on-Thames, Surrey.

Vintage thespian F. L. Lyndhurst, at the age of 81, had established a glass-house studio beside the beach at Shoreham, Sussex. His protégés, the Progress Film Company, took on *The Mayor of Casterbridge* in February 1921. Producer and director Sidney Morgan visited Max Gate to discuss script corrections, particularly dialect 'titles' (the words that captioned silent films) with the author in April 1921. He also asked for advice on locations. These included Maiden Castle at dawn and the actors and crew would arrive at the King's Arms Hotel at one o'clock in the morning of 2 July 1921. Fred Groves and Pauline Peters were Mr and Mrs Henchard. Fragments exist of the 'sold' wife meeting the Mayor in ancient earthworks and of Elizabeth Jane and her lover beside Hangman's Cottage.

Hardy's own account, written in the third person under his wife's name, shows how Dorchester people took the filming in their stride:

'Although the actors had their faces coloured yellow and were dressed in the fashion of 80 years earlier, Hardy observed, to his surprise, that the townspeople passed by on their ordinary affairs and seemed not to notice the strange spectacle, nor did any interest seem aroused when Hardy drove through the town with the actors to Maiden Castle, that ancient earthwork which formed the background to one part of the film.'

The first Hardy among the talkies was *Under the Greenwood Tree*, an adaptation with folk-songs as well as dialogue sound, though it would not be released until 1929, after the author was dead. *Far From the Madding Crowd*, the 1967 classic by John Schlesinger, will probably remain an all-time perfect production, given that it used more Dorset and Wessex locations than all the other Hardy productions of the twentieth century put together. Few coincided with those in the book but that was inevitable given the extent to which Hardy's rural idyll had already been compromised.

Tess would be refilmed after Roman Polanski paid the Selznick estate $25,000 for a reversion of the rights. For legal reasons it could not be filmed in countries that might enforce extradition proceedings, in relation to a case in the United States, and the Bagshot Beds geology of Brittany came up with unspoilt and appealingly rustic visions of the Dorset heaths as they would have looked a century earlier. *Jude*, directed by Michael Winterbottom in 1996, was acclaimed for its 'visually remarkable adaptation' (though filmed in New Zealand and the Yorkshire Dales, not that much of Hardy's last novel takes place in Dorset). It starred Christopher Eccleston in the lead role, with Kate Winslet giving a 'mesmerising performance' as Sue, his vivacious cousin and illicit lover.

The other twentieth-century contribution to culture was war poetry. Hardy excelled at it, with his natural depressive moods being fed by the carnage on the Western Front and brought home by the fear that the Kaiser would succeed where Napoleon had failed. For a time it seemed quite possible that the Germans might land on the Dorset coast. Hardy's poems have been seen as a protest against the war but they are not the work of a pacifist.

He deplored the truce in No Man's Land, supported conscription as an inevitability, and urged the 'crushing utterly' of Irish rebels.

Childless themselves, Tom and Florence talked of finding a 'Hardy-born' heir - he was now the richest author in the country - and decided to adopt young barrister Frank George. The son of cousin Angelina Hardy from Puddletown and William George, landlord of the Royal Oak Inn in Bere Regis, he was born there on 5 December 1880. Called to the bar, on 17 November 1913, he was in rooms at Gray's Inn in The Temple and passed muster as 'the only decent relation'.

Fate intervened in a horribly Hardyesque way. Second-Lieutenant Frank William George of the 5th Battalion of the Dorsetshire Regiment fell in a bayonet attack on the Turkish front trench across the Valley of Death below Hetman Chair in the Gallipoli peninsula on 21 August 1915.

Tom's beloved sister Mary also died, of emphysema, on 24 November 1915. Her failure to make a will put Tom in control of probate as next-of-kin, causing a rift in the dysfunctional Hardy family with brother Henry swearing at Tom and sister Kate reduced to moody silence. The discord marred the funeral and hardened the family's hostility to Florence who they feared would walk off with the author's riches. Hardy took refuge in his study, producing some of his most intense poems as a retreat into memory, and was now almost a recluse in Dorchester. 'My reminiscences; no, never!' he told Sir George Douglas in December 1915. Finding it agonising to read old letters and documents, he gathered odd thoughts for his poems, and then destroyed them: 'They raise ghosts.'

In the awful middle of the war, in September 1916, he took Florence on a visit from Emma's Plymouth birthplace to meet her Launceston cousins and see the monument he had designed in St Juliot church. Florence, who was often unwell, confessed to 'home worries, of a kind to break down any woman's nerve'. This included strife with the domestic servants and the cook at Max Gate was often only minutes away from walking out. The Hardys also managed to engineer a totally unnecessary rift with their oldest and wealthiest mutual friend. They feared Edward Clodd's forthcoming *Memories* might disclose their secrets but in the event they were 'so dull' that nothing was revealed. It was doubly unfortunate that his place was taken by opportunistic Sydney Cockerell from the Fitzwilliam Museum at Cambridge who talked his way into becoming Hardy's literary executor.

Hardy and Florence experienced a Zeppelin attack on London from J. M. Barrie's flat. This led H. G. Wells to tell Virginia Woolf that Hardy had visited London specially to see an air-raid. Tom was indignant when he heard the story from Virginia:

'What things they say! I was with my wife. There was an air-raid one night when we stayed with Barrie. We just heard a little pop in the distance. The searchlights were beautiful. I thought if a bomb now were to fall on this flat how many writers would be lost.'

Touchingly, on publication of *Moments of Vision*, Hardy inscribed the 'first copy of the first edition, to the first of women Florence Hardy'. It ends with the wonderful poem 'Afterwards' in which Hardy writes his own obituary as 'a man who used to notice such things' with memorable images such as the hedgehog furtively crossing the lawn.

Tom never drove or owned a motor car but regularly hired a dark blue Mercedes Benz and chauffeur from Tilley's Garage in Dorchester. His drivers were Bob Scott, Dick Shipton and, for preference, Lionel Voss, after the latter joined the firm at the age of 21 in 1912. The car was generally booked through the summer for each Monday and Thursday, for a drive and picnic in the Dorset countryside. Regular stopping points included Badbury Rings, the Cross and Hand (Batcombe), the Hardy Monument, Holme Lane (Stoborough), and Lydlinch Common. Favourite thatched public houses were the Crown Inn, at Marnhull, and the Royal Yeoman at Grimstone, before the latter was rebuilt:

'This inn caught fire and was burnt to the ground and the next day I had to motor Hardy over to see the ruins. He stood in front of it looking very sad and thoughtful. The inn was rebuilt without a thatched roof, but his interest had gone and never again did he want to stop and look.'

The last known outing was to Ilminster in October 1927. Voss recalled these trips in the pamphlet *Motoring with Thomas Hardy* which James Stevens Cox published in 1963:

'He liked an open touring car and disliked fast driving. Twenty-five miles per hour was the fastest speed he would allow me to travel. He always sat in front with me and chatted about the places we visited, and the houses and inns we passed. During the drives he frequently spoke of incidents in his younger days, as the place or scene reminded him.'

Social visits included dropping in on Sir Cecil Hanbury (1871-1937) and his daughter

Caroline, at Kingston Maurward House, and C. H. St John Hornby (1867-1946), founder of the Ashendene Press and director of W. H. Smith & Son Limited, at Chantmarle.

Hardy's eightieth birthday in 1920, bringing 200 congratulatory telegrams, prompted Florence to mount a campaign to persuade Tom to modernise Max Gate. It was no longer acceptable, she argued, for it to be the only big house in Dorchester without a bathroom. Well-pumped water was still being heated in saucepans in front of the fire and poured into a hip-bath. Tom was in the running for the Nobel Prize for Literature but had to be satisfied with an honorary D.Lit from Oxford University. In advanced old age his lifelong sensitivity to criticism reached an acute state of obsessive overreaction which spoilt much of the media attention he received.

A new generation of poets and writers revered him. To Siegfried Sassoon he was 'the Wessex Wizard'. W. M. Parker, author of the *Letters of Sir Walter Scott*, visited Max Gate in September 1920 and described Hardy as 'the great little Wizard of the South'. Sir James Barrie came in May 1921 and the pair of them walked across the meadows to the Bockhampton birthplace where the writer Hermann Lea had been staying. They found it deserted and locked. Barrie was determined to see inside so they broke in through a window. 'The Fallow Deer at the Lonely House' resulted from another wave of nostalgia.

Sir Newman Flower, the publisher, described Hardy's physical appearance as:

'. . . a very little man, with a great dome forehead. A very little man with a pricked moustache, and deep-set eyes, a curved nose, and small white hands with short stubby fingers. I have never yet seen what I would regard as the perfect photograph of Hardy. But a Russian sculptor named [Serge] Yourievitch made a bust of him in 1924 which has always seemed to me the best portrait. The sculptor beat the camera.'

Hardy himself remarked:

'The Russian has put in that large curved nose without mercy.'

As for its shape, Virginia Woolf found the words for it:

'His nose had a joint in it and the end curved down.'

Hardy's 'favourite walk' from Max Gate, with Wessex the terrier, was down Syward Road and across the railway line and the River Frome, then over the meadows to visit the family graves in Stinsford churchyard. Sometimes he continued to Kingston Maurward. Despite a serious kidney malfunction in February 1922 he resumed cycling and visited Kate and Henry in Talbothays Lodge, the villa he had designed for them in West Stafford. Talbothays turned another of his imaginary placenames into a real name on the map.

He worked on a play, *The Famous Tragedy of the Queen of Cornwall* for his favourite actress, Mrs Gertrude Bugler, and received visits from old friends Florence Henniker and Lady Agnes Grove. Mrs Henniker died in April 1923. The artist Augustus John, living at Poole, captured the image of Hardy with the ageless dignity of a great Victorian.

More than anything else, his lasting reputation in Dorchester was secured by a royal visitor, on 20 July 1923. Edward, Prince of Wales - the future King Edward VIII - called to

Talbothays Lodge, West Stafford, was designed by Thomas Hardy and built by brother Henry for their sister Kate

South Dorset's other literary shrine, at Clouds Hill, where Mr and Mrs Hardy visited Lawrence of Arabia

Lawrence of Arabia – subsequently living down the 'Prince of Mecca' image – became a frequent guest at Max Gate

take him on a tour through the county town which was followed by lunch at Max Gate. The locals were also impressed by regular appearances on a Brough Superior motorcycle of national hero Lawrence of Arabia, Colonel Thomas Edward Lawrence - alias Private Shaw of the Royal Tank Corps - from Bovington Camp. Arriving 'like a thunderbolt', on his Brough Superior motor-cycle, he 'utterly captivated' Hardy. They shared a friendship with the author E. M. Forster. Florence and Tom visited Lawrence's spartan cottage at Clouds Hill which now completes the trio of south Dorset literary properties owned by the National Trust.

A pro-Soviet visitor, in June 1924, was the composer Rutland Boughton (1878-1960) who spent a couple of days at Max Gate. Though he persuaded conservative Hardy to allow him to perform a musical version of *The Queen of Cornwall* at Glastonbury Abbey he utterly failed to convert him to communism.

Hardy finally achieved his aim of proving that poetry could be a best-seller, having his revenge over past critics on 20 November 1925. *Human Shows, Far Phantasies*, in a first edition of 5,000 copies, sold out within hours. Everyone now wrote glowingly about him. To Leonard Woolf he was 'the spiritual parent' of modern poets. With Leonard, wife Virginia Woolf visited 'the puffy-cheeked cheerful old man' at Max Gate on Sunday 25 July 1926. He was 'dressed in rough grey with a striped tie', his eyes 'now faded and rather watery'. Hardy recalled seeing Virginia in her cradle 'at Hyde Park Place - oh, Gate was it'. Wessex the dog interrupted the discussion on poetry and they discussed various friends, notably Colonel Lawrence. 'I hope he won't commit suicide,' Mrs Hardy said. 'He promised me not to go into the air,' Hardy said, referring to Lawrence enlisting in the Royal Air Force, though as an Aircraftman on the ground. 'My husband doesn't like anything to do with the air,' Florence explained, as the unruly dog demanded. It is with relief that Virginia Woolf tells us: 'Wessex went wheezing away.'

Visiting Lady Hester Pinney at Racedown, near Broadwindsor, in 1925 and again when entertaining Mr and Mrs John Galsworthy at Max Gate in 1927, Hardy left a darker abiding memory. He talked in detail about public hangings. There was also a relaxation of his natural reserve and resistance at meeting a wider audience. Having attended John

Below right: Wessex guarding the door in Hardy's 1923 Christmas card

Below left: Wessex in December 1926, the month he died, accosting the postman at Max Gate

MAX GATE. DORCHESTER. XMAS. 1926.   WITH THE THOUGHTS OF T.H. & F.E.H.

GREETINGS - - - from Mr. and Mrs. THOMAS HARDY

Max Gate. Dorchester.   Xmas. 1923

119

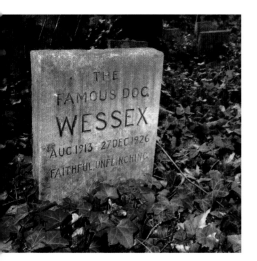

The stone to 'Famous Dog Wessex' in the pets' cemetery at Max Gate

Drinkwater's adaptation of *The Mayor of Casterbridge*, on stage in Weymouth on 20 September 1926, he received a standing ovation. He also laid the foundation stone of the new Dorchester Grammar School - cementing the Thomas Hardye and Thomas Hardy connection, as he put it - on 21 July 1927. Literary locations were confirmed for posterity after young calligrapher and illustrator Heather Child (1911-97) met Hardy. She produced the decorated map which is now displayed in Dorset County Museum.

Two deaths affected him greatly. Agnes Grove died on 7 December 1926. Then, on the 27th, he was parted from his best friend. 'The Famous Dog Wessex - Faithful, unflinching', to quote his gravestone, lies in the pets' cemetery at Max Gate. The rough-haired terrier was born in August 1913 and they had shared 'thousands of afternoons'. Lady Grove and Wessex each had commemorative poems - 'Concerning Agnes' and 'Dead Wessex the Dog to the Household'. Hardy's achievement in old age, as biographer Robert Gittings observed, was to go on writing, as prolific and poignant as ever. The impetus, however, was primarily the loss of love 'then all mourning, mourning'.

Hardy's last contribution to national events was to broadcast 'A Wessex Programme' for the BBC from Bournemouth on 30 December 1926. His life gradually drew to a close from 11 December 1927, in bed at Max Gate with Dr Gowring coming through the snow to diagnose 'old age', and Sydney Cockerell and Sir James Barrie preparing to tell the world. Tom kept them waiting, for a full month, until the evening of 11 January 1928.

The previous evening he had asked Florence to read him Robert Browning's poem 'Rabbi Ben Ezra' in its entirety. At dusk on the 11th he chose *The Rubaiyat of Omar Khayyam* but could only concentrate for a single verse. He began to lose consciusness and died of a heart attack at about nine o'clock.

Cockerell and Barrie conspired to pressure Florence into thwarting Tom's wishes. Back in 1924, Hardy had written to Stinsford's vicar, Revd Henry Guise Beatson Cowley:

'Yes, regard me as a parishioner certainly. I hope to be still more one when I am in a supine position some day.'

Instead they arranged a Westminster Abbey funeral - overruling the combined pleas of Florence, Kate and Henry - with his heart being removed by Dorchester surgeon Edward Weller Mann for Stinsford burial and the body being taken in Grassbys' hearse to Woking Crematorium. From there it was an urn-burial that went to London.

Above left: His heart in Wessex, shaded by a yew tree, in Stinsford churchyard

Above middle: The author's first memorial was a granite oblelisk erected beside Hardy's Cottage by 'a few of his American admirers' in 1931

Above: Sundial commemorating Hardy's years at Max Gate (1885 to 1928), added after his death

Left: Eric Kennington's statue looks westwards from Top o' Town at Dorchester

The compromise was a 'staggering blow' to Kate Hardy, offending as it did against the old country belief that bodies should be buried intact, and even cosmopolitan friends like Edward Clodd found it 'repellent'. Hardy's publisher Sir Daniel Macmillan and his secretary compounded the agony, by sending out invitations to the Abbey service almost at random, turning the occasion into 'a sick horror' for Florence. 'Today the ashes of Hardy lie but a few feet away from Dickens,' Newman Flower reflected. 'Two great writers who met but never spoke.'

He left more than £90,000 - all of it from his writings - which was a fortune for the time. Former domestic servants saw the irony in this and were muttering for years about the meagre household budget, as they catalogued Hardy's miserly idiosyncrasies, such as removing coal from the fire for future use.

BBC 'experimental' radio station 5GB, live from Birmingham on the Daventry transmitter gave the first broadcast of *Tess*, the opera by Baron Frederic d'Erlanger, at eight o'clock in the evening of Saturday 2 March 1929. The libretto, by Luigi Illica, was translated into English by Alfred Kalisch. The performance lasted more than 2 hours 15 minutes and was followed by the daily weather forecast and news bulletin.

Conventional memorials followed, including that in Poet's Corner, and a stained-glass window in Stinsford church. Augustus John offered his vision of Tess, as a sculpture, but that was turned down. Sydney Cockerell wanted a second Hardy Monument, on the heath behind his birthplace, but American book collector A. E. Newton beat him to it with a 10-feet granite column in the style of a war memorial. It was placed rather incongruously under the beech trees between Hardy's Cottage and his favourite Snail Creep path. John Livingston Lowes unveiled it on behalf of the 'American friends'.

Somewhat better, peering westwards from Colliton Walk at Top o' Town, Dorchester, is Eric Kennington's bronze statue of a seated Hardy. It was unveiled by Sir James Barrie on 2 September 1931 with a speech of characteristic puckishness that dismayed Florence: 'There were years when I thought him the most unhappy man I had ever known.' It was true but hardly adequate for the occasion of revealing his lasting likeness to a cynical world. A contemporary comment summed it up:

'Criticism must be withheld, as it doubtless pleased the committee and subscribers who were responsible for its erection.'

Derelict at the time of his death, the ancient church at Winterborne Tomson was restored in Hardy's memory

Altar, pulpit and box-pews in the simple single-cell church at Winterborne Tomson

The Society for the Preservation of Ancient Buildings, through its former secretary Albert Reginald Powys - brother of the literary trio John Cowper, Theodore and Llewelyn - sold some Hardy papers and used the cash to restore Winterborne Tomson church in his memory. Hardy wrote that this simple little building, near Bere Regis, had been left 'just as it was when the parishioners went out of it fifty years ago after the last service'.

Florence without Thomas must have seemed a lost soul as she fought rearguard battles against those who had belittled his reputation. More constructively she now enjoyed perfect relations with brother-in-law Henry until he followed Tom on 9 December 1928. In the new decade, Florence played a leading role in removing the slums from Mixen Lane, as her husband called it, replacing them with modern flats through Mill Street Housing Society. Prime Minister Ramsay MacDonald visited her and discussed the project. Her companions now were her French bulldogs with Toby being succeeded by Tobina. Florence had suffered various ear, nose and throat problems for many years and succumbed to cancer of the rectum on 17 October 1937.

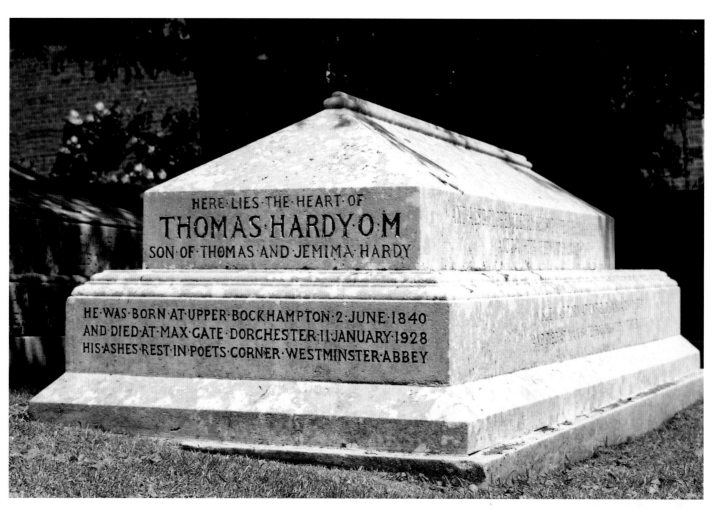

Stinsford churchyard - his heart in Wessex

Only Kate was left. A cousin, Nathaniel Sparks (died 1961) - an artist and engraver from Puddletown whose principal work is in Bristol City Museum and Art Gallery - cared for her in advanced old age. Nathaniel was the grandson of Tom and Kate's maternal aunt, Maria Sparks.

Kate Hardy rounded off the Hardy story by seeing that his study was reconstructed inside Dorset County Museum at Dorchester and also ensured that Max Gate passed to the National Trust, plus provision of sufficient additional funds for the purchase of the Bockhampton birthplace. This was bought by the National Trust in 1948. A second acre was added to the garden of Hardy's Cottage in 1967.

Thomas Hardy's study from Max Gate, complete with furniture and books, was reassembled in Dorset County Museum

The 1590 date-stone (top)
of the Old Mill, Fordington,
rebuilt in 1940 as a result
of Florence Hardy's work for
Mill Street Housing Society

The Hardy shrine in Dorset
County Museum

East of Max Gate, now separated from it by the A35 bypass, The Trumpet Major public house was opened by ex-Prime Minister and head of Hardy's publishers Harold Macmillan, as part of the Thomas Hardy Festival on 9 July 1968. The Japanese contingent, finding a particular empathy with the author's mood, were the most conspicuous overseas visitors. There was a Thomas Hardy Society in Japan long before one was established in England. Knowledge of Hardy's Wessex - from Cornwall to the Thames - is now being revived by an active Thomas Hardy Fellowship led by stalwart Hardyan John Pentney from Taunton.

Hardy scholar Frank Pinion (1908-97), a teacher from Whitehaven, Nottingham and finally Sheffield, produced a series of studies on the author's poems and friendships. The everyday memories of servants and the Dorset populace were gathered by Guernsey bookseller James Stevens Cox in a collection of 35 monographs that formed the source material for D. F. Barber's *Concerning Thomas Hardy*. Perhaps the finest tribute to the calibre of Hardy's poems, from one of his peers, came when Philip Larkin chose 27 of them for inclusion in *The Oxford Book of Twentieth-Century Verse*.

Kate Hardy died during the Battle of Britain on 4 October 1940. Thomas Hardy's centenary had been overshadowed by national events but an ex-Premier, Lord Baldwin, laid the commemorative wreath in Dorchester during that first summer of the Second World War. Having returned home from earlier eulogistic speeches, Kate Hardy left us this enigmatic thought:

'If they only knew!'

Gazeteer of Hardy Locations

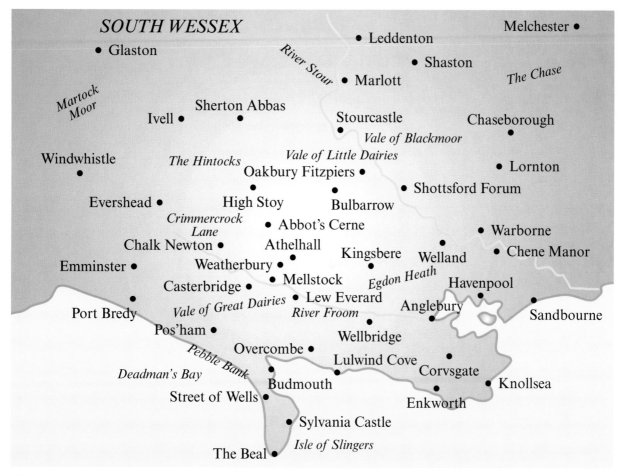

Map showing Hardy's Dorset

Abbey Walk, Shaston = itself, Abbey Walk, Shaftesbury, Dorset

Abbot's Cernel = Cerne Abbas, Dorset

Abbotsea = Abbotsbury, Dorset

Aldbrickham = Reading, Berkshire

Alderworth = Briantspuddle, Dorset

Alfredston = Wantage, Berkshire

Ancient West Highway = Roman road from Winterbourne Abbas to Eggardon Hill in west Dorset

Anglebury = Wareham, Dorset

Anglebury Heath = Northport Heath and Great Ovens Hill, Wareham, Dorset

Antelope Hotel, Casterbridge = itself, Antelope Hotel (now a shopping precinct), Dorchester, Dorset

Antelope Inn, Nuttlebury = itself, Antelope Inn, Hazelbury Bryan, Dorset

Aquae Sulis = itself, being the Roman name for Bath, Somerset

Arrowthorne Lodge = Minstead Lodge, near Lyndhurst, Hampshire

Athelhall = Athelhampton Hall, near Puddletown, Dorset

Back Street, Casterbridge = Trinity Street, Dorchester, Dorset

Baden = itself, the Grand-Duchy of Baden, in Germany

Badger's Clump = Chydyok Farm, Chaldon Herring, Dorset

Bank Walks = itself, Bank Walk between Lower Bockhampton and Stinsford, Dorset

Barnes's Lane = itself, Barnes's Lane bridleway between Alton Pancras and Buckland Newton, Dorset

Barrow Beacon = itself, on Beacon Hill, Puddletown, Dorset

Barwith Strand = Trebarwith Strand, near Tintagel, Cornwall

Batten Castle = Lulworth Castle, East Lulworth, Dorset

Bath = itself, Bath, Somerset

The Beal = Pulpit Rock, Portland Bill, Dorset

Beal Lantern = pre-1905 Portland Bill Lighthouse, now the Bird Observatory, Portland, Dorset

The Bear, Alfredston = itself, the Bear Hotel, Wantage, Oxfordshire

Bede's Inn, London = Clement's Inn, London WC2

Beeny Cliff = itself, Beeny Cliff, near Boscastle, Cornwall

Beersheba, Christminster = Jericho district of inner-city Oxford

Belvidere Hotel, Budmouth = itself, Belvedere Private Hotel (now The Sands Hotel), 117-118 The Esplanade, Weymouth, Dorset

Benvill Lane = itself, Benville Lane, near Evershot, Dorset

Biblioll College, Christminster = Balliol College, Oxford

Bimport Street = itself, Bimport, Shaftesbury, Dorset

(The) Birthplace = itself, Hardy's Cottage, Veterans' Alley (now Cherry Lane), Higher Bockhampton, Stinsford, Dorset

Black Bull Hotel, Port Bredy = Bull Hotel, East Street, Bridport, Dorset

Black'on = itself, Black Down (with Admiral Hardy's Monument), Portesham, Dorset

Blackmoor Vale = itself, though now generally spelt Blackmore Vale, across north Dorset

Bloom's End = Bhompston Farm, between Lower Bockhampton and Norris Mill, Stinsford, Dorset

Bossiney = itself, Bossiney, near Boscastle, Cornwall

Bottom Pond = Rimsmoor Pond, south of Briantspuddle, Dorset

Bowling Walk, Casterbridge = Bowling Alley Walk, Dorchester

Bramshurst Manor = Moyles Court (now Moyles Court School), near Ringwood, Hampshire

Bredy Knap = itself, Bredy Knap (on the A35) above Long Bredy, Dorset

Bristol = itself, Bristol

Broad Sidlinch = Sydling St Nicholas, Dorset

Brown House = Red House, between Fawley and Wantage, Berkshire

Bubb Down = itself, Bubb Down Hill, Melbury Bubb, Dorset

Buck's Head = former inn at Troytown, near Puddletown, Dorset

Buckbury Fitzpiers = Okeford Fitzpaine (renamed Oakbury Fitzpiers for the later novels), Dorset

Budmouth = Weymouth, Dorset

Budmouth Barracks = Red Barracks (now Wellington Court), Barrack Road, Weymouth, Dorset

Budmouth Custom House = itself, the Custom House, Custom House Quay, Weymouth, Dorset

Budmouth Regis = Melcombe Regis, Weymouth, Dorset

Bulbarrow = itself, Bulbarrow Hill, central Dorset

Bull Stake Square, Casterbridge = itself, Bull Stake Square (now known as North Square), Dorchester, Dorset

Buttock's Spring = water-splash at Melbury Osmond, Dorset

Camelot = Cadbury Castle, South Cadbury, Somerset

Canning's Basin, Liverpool = Canning Dock, Liverpool

Camelton = Camelford, Cornwall

Cardinal College, Christminster = Christ Church College, Oxford

Cardinal Street, Christminster = St Aldate's Street, Oxford

Carriford = West Stafford, Dorset

Carriford Road = Crossways, Dorset

Carriford Road Station = Moreton Station, near Crossways, Dorset

Casterbridge = Dorchester, Dorset

Casterbridge Barracks = itself, the former Marabout Barracks, Poundbury Road, Dorchester, Dorset

Casterbridge Gaol = itself, Dorchester Prison, North Square, Dorchester, Dorset

Casterbridge Grammar School = itself, the former Dorchester Grammar School, South Street, Dorchester, Dorset

Casterbridge Museum = itself, Dorset County Museum, High West Street, Dorchester, Dorset

Casterbridge Station = itself, Dorchester (South) Station, Dorchester, Dorset

Casterbridge Workhouse = itself, the former Dorchester Union Workhouse, Damer's Road (facing junction with Maud Road), Dorchester, Dorset

Castle Boterel = Boscastle, Cornwall

Castle Boterel Inn = former Ship Inn, Valency Road, Boscastle, Cornwall

Castle Inn = itself, the Castle Inn (demolished in the 1920s), 7 Middle Street, Yeovil, Somerset

Castle Royal = Windsor Castle, Berkshire

Catknoll Street = Chetnole, Dorset

Cerne = itself, Cerne Abbas, Dorset

Cernel = Cerne Abbas, Dorset

Chaldon = itself, West Chaldon, near Lulworth, Dorset

Chaldon Down = itself, above West Chaldon and East Chaldon, near Lulworth, Dorset

Chalk Newton = Maiden Newton, Dorset

Chalk Walk, Casterbridge = Colliton Walk, Dorchester, Dorset

Charmley = Charminster, Dorset

Chaseborough = Cranborne, Dorset

The Chase = Cranborne Chase, Dorset and Wiltshire

Chasetown = alternative for Cranborne, Dorset

Chateau Ringdale = house at Allington, Bridport, moved by Hardy to Harbour Road, West Bay, Bridport, Dorset

Cheltenham = itself, Cheltenham, Gloucestershire

Chene Manor = Canford Manor (now Canford School), near Wimborne, Dorset

Chesil Bank = itself, Chesil Beach, between Abbotsbury and Portland, Dorset

Chief Street, Christminster = High Street, Oxford

Chillington Wood = Killerton Clump, Broadclyst, near Exeter, Devon

Christminster = Oxford

Church 'with the Italian porch', Christminster = St Mary the Virgin, Oxford

Cirque of the Gladiators, Casterbridge = Maumbury Rings, Dorchester, Dorset

Clammers Gate = itself, Clammers Gate, into Melbury Park from Town's End, Melbury Osmond, Dorset

Classical Mansion = Wilton House, near Salisbury, Wiltshire

Clavinium = 'Clavino' of the Ravenna Cosmography, which Hardy applied to the Roman temple on Jordan Hill, Preston, near Weymouth, Dorset

Cliff 'without a name' = High Cliff, Pentargon Bay, Cornwall

Cliff Martin = Combe Martin, Devon

Clifton Horseleigh = Clifton Maybank, near Sherborne, Dorset

The Close, Melchester = itself, The Close, Salisbury, Wiltshire

Cloton = Chedington or Clapton, west of Corscombe, in the Dorset-Somerset borderlands

Clyffe Hill Clump = itself, Clyffe Hill Clump, Tincleton, Dorset

Conquer Barrow = itself, Conquer Barrow, behind Casterbridge Road (near Max Gate), Dorchester. Dorset

Coomb Barn = itself, Coombe Barn, south-west of Puddletown, Dorset

Coomb Eweleaze = sheep pasture on White Hill, Puddletown, Dorset

Corn Street, Casterbridge = South Street and Cornhill, Dorchester, Dorset

Corvsgate = village of Corfe Castle, Dorset

Corvsgate Castle = the castle at Corfe Castle, Dorset

Court House, Casterbridge = Shire Hall, High West Street, Dorchester, Dorset

Cove Row, Budmouth = itself, harbourside Cove Row, Weymouth, Dorset

Cresscombe = Letcombe Bassett, near Wantage, Oxfordshire

Creston = Preston, near Weymouth, Dorset

Crimmercrock Lane = Cromlech Crock Road (now the A356), across Toller Down, near Maiden Newton, Dorset

Cripplegate Church = St Mary-le-Bow Church, Cheapside, London EC2

Cross-in-Hand = Cross and Hand wayside stone, near Batcombe, Dorset

Crossy Hand = also the Cross and Hand, near Batcombe, Dorset

Crown Hotel, Shottsford Forum = itself, Crown Hotel, Blandford Forum, Dorset

Crown Inn, Marlott = itself, The Crown, Marnhull, Dorset

Crozier College, Christminster = Oriel College, Oxford

Crozier Hotel, Christminster = Mitre Hotel, Oxford

Cuckoo Lane, Mellstock = itself, Cuckoo Lane (south from A35), Higher Bockhampton, Stinsford, Dorset

Dagger's Grave = Daggers Gate, near Newland Farm, West Lulworth, Dorset

de Stancy Castle = Dunster Castle, Dunster, Somerset

Deadman's Bay = Chesil Cove, Portland, and Lyme Bay, Dorset

Deansleigh Park = Broadlands House, near Romsey, Hampshire

Delborough = East Chelborough, near Evershot, Dorset

Devil's Bellows = Culpepper's Dish, near Briantspuddle, Dorset

Devil's Door = Devil's Den, Clatford Bottom, Fyfield, Marlborough, Wiltshire

Devil's Kitchen = itself, the Devil's Kitchen on the northern slope of High Stoy, Minterne Magna, Dorset

Dogbury Hill = itself, Dogbury Hill, Minterne Magna, Dorset

Dole Hill = itself, Dole's Hill, Piddlehinton, Dorset

Downstaple = Barnstaple, Devon

Dree-armed Cross = three-armed direction post at the road junction west of Stafford House, West Stafford, Dorset

Druid Stone = itself, in the garden of Max Gate, Dorchester

Duke's Arms, Shaston = Grosvenor Arms (those of the Duke of Westminster), Shaftesbury, Dorset

Dundagel = Tintagel, Cornwall

Dunkery Tor = itself, Dunkery Beacon, near Minehead, Somerset

Durnover = Fordington, Dorchester, Dorset

Durnover Great Field = Fordington Field across the site of the Prince of Wales's Poundbury development, Dorchester, Dorset

Durnover Green = The Green, Fordington, Dorchester, Dorset

Durnover Hill = Fordington Hill, Dorchester, Dorset

Durnover Hole = weir-pool on River Frome, downstream from Grey's Bridge, Dorchester, Dorset

Durnover Lea = water-meadows at Fordington, Dorchester, Dorset

Durnover Mill = East Mills, Mill Street, Fordington, Dorchester, Dorset

Durnover Moor = water-meadows between Fordington and Stinsford, near Dorchester, Dorset

Earl of Wessex Hotel, Sherton Abbas = former Digby Hotel, Digby Road, Sherborne, Dorset (now The Digby dormitories of Sherborne School)

East Egdon = Affpuddle and Briantspuddle, Dorset

East Endelstow = Lesnewth, near Boscastle, Cornwall

East Mellstock = Lower Bockhampton, Stinsford, Dorset

East Quarriers = Grove Cliff group of quarries (namely France, High Headlands, Broadcroft, Yeolands and Silklake Quarries), Portland, Dorset

Eastern village = Easton, Portland, Dorset

Egdon Heath = heathland from Stinsford eastwards to Turners Puddle, Dorset

Eggar = Eggardon Hill, near Askerswell, Dorset

Elensford = Duddle Farm, near Stinsford (though just inside 'the adjoining parish' of Puddletown, as Hardy notes), Dorset

Elm Cranlynch = Corfe Mullen, Dorset

Emminster = Beaminster, Dorset

Endelstow = St Juliot, near Boscastle, Cornwall

Endelstow House = house in the valley of the River Valency, near Boscastle, Cornwall

Enkworth Court = Encombe House, Kingston, near Corfe Castle, Dorset

Evershead = Evershot, Dorset

Ewelease Stile = that on the path between Higher Bockhampton and Stinsford, Dorset

Exon Moor = Exmoor, Devon and Somerset

Exonbury = Exeter, Devon
Exonbury Crescent = this Exeter Crescent was an invented address in central London

Falcon Hotel = White Hart Hotel, Launceston, Cornwall
Falmouth = itself, Falmouth, Cornwall
Falls Park = Mells Park, near Frome, Somerset
(The) Fane = temple-style gazebo near the lake, Kingston Maurward, near Stinsford, Dorset
Farnfield = Farnborough, Hampshire
Fensworth = village near Fawley, Berkshire
Fernell Hall = Embley House (now Embley Park School), near Romsey, Hampshire
Field of tombs, Casterbridge = Dorchester Cemetery, Weymouth Road, Dorchester, Dorset
Flintcombe Ash = Dole's Ash and Plush, near Piddletrenthide, Dorset
Flower-de-Luce, Chaseborough = Fluer-de-Lis, Cranborne, Dorset
Flychett = Lytchett Minster, near Poole, Dorset
Fonthill = itself, Fonthill Abbey, near Tisbury, Wiltshire
Forest of the White Hart = King's Stag, near Lydlinch, Dorset
Forum = Blandford Forum, Dorset
Fountall = Wells, Somerset
Fountall Cathedral = Wells Cathedral, Wells, Somerset
Fountall Theological College = Wells Theological College, Wells, Somerset
Fourways, Christminster = Carfax (corrupted French for crossroads), Oxford
Froom = River Frome (pronounced Froom), Dorset
Froom Everard = Frome Billet, West Stafford, Dorset
Froom Everard House = Stafford House, West Stafford, Dorset
Froom River = River Frome, Dorset
Frome Side Vale = Frome Valley, Dorset

Gaymead = Shinfield, near Reading, Berkshire
Giant o' Cernel = Cerne Giant, Cerne Abbas, Dorset
Giant's Town = Hugh Town, St Mary's, Isles of Scilly
Gibraltar of Wessex = Portland, Dorset
Glaston = itself, Glaston being the milestone contraction for Glastonbury, Somerset
Gloucester Lodge, Budmouth = itself, now Gloucester Hotel, Gloucester Row, 85 The Esplande, Weymouth, Dorset
Great Forest = New Forest, Hampshire
Great Grey Plain = Salisbury Plain, Wiltshire

Great Hintock = Minterne Magna, Dorset

Great Hintock House = Minterne House, Minterne Magna, Dorset

Great Mid-Wessex Plain = Salisbury Plain, Wiltshire

(The) Great Plain = also Salisbury Plain, Wiltshire

Great Pool = weir on the River Frome, Woodsford, Dorset

Green Hill, Kingsbere = Woodbury Hill, Bere Regis, Dorset

Green Hill Fair, Kingsbere = Woodbury Hill Fair, Bere Regis, Dorset

Grey's Bridge, Casterbridge = itself, Grey's Bridge, Dorchester, Dorset

Grey's Wood = itself, Grey's Wood, Higher Kingston, near Stinsford, Dorset

Haggardon Hill = Eggardon Hill, near Askerswell, Dorset

Hangman's Cottage, Casterbridge = itself, Hangman's Cottage, Glyde Path Road, Dorchester, Dorset

Harbour Inn, Port Bredy = Bridport Arms Hotel, West Bay, Bridport, Dorset

Havenpool = Poole, Dorset

Heath Plantation Hill = the hill between Warmwell and Crossways, Dorset

Heedless William's Pond = itself, Heedless William's Pond, beside Duddle Heath, near Stinsford, Dorset

Hendford Hill = itself, Hendford Hill, Yeovil, Somerset

Henry the Eighth's Castle = Sandsfoot Castle, Weymouth, Dorset

Henstridge Cross = Virginia Ash, Henstridge, Somerset

Hermitage = itself, Hermitage, Dorset

Heymere House = Clevedon Court, Clevedon, Somerset

High Place Hall, Casterbridge = Colliton House, Glyde Path Road, Dorchester, Dorset

High-Stoy Hill = itself, High Stoy Hill, Minterne Magna, Dorset

High Street, Casterbridge = High East Street and High West Street, Dorchester, Dorset

High Street, Havenpool = itself, high Street, Poole, Dorset

Higher Crowstairs = Waterston Ridge, near Puddletown, Dorset

Hintock = a Hardy name that has moved from fiction into fact, being adopted for a telephone exchange covering the southern Blackmore Vale, Dorset

Hintock Green = Milddlemarsh, Minterne Magna, Dorset

Hintock House = Turnworth House, Turnworth, Dorset

Hintocks = countryside around Bubb Down Hill and High Stoy between Melbury Osmond and Minterne Magna, Dorset

Hocbridge = amalgam of Hoccum and Stourbridge, for a town in the West Midlands

Hollow Hill = itself, being the local name for the rise between Bockhampton Cross and Higher Bockhampton, Stinsford, Dorset

Holway = itself, Holway Lane, from Cattistock to Evershot, Dorset

Holloway Lane = also Holway Lane, from Cattistock to Evershot, Dorset

Holmstoke = amalgam of East Stoke and East Holme, Dorset

Holworth = itself, Holworth, near Owermoigne, Dorset

Hope Church = St Andrew's Church (ruin), Church Ope Cove, Portland, Dorset

Hyde Park Glass-house = itself, the former Crystal Palace, Hyde Park, London

Icen Way = Roman road across Puddletown Heath. near Puddletown, Dorset

Icenway House = Hackwood House, Winslade, near Basingstoke, Hampshire

Idmouth = Sidmouth, Devon

Ikling Way = Ackling Dyke Roman road, to Salisbury and London, from Badbury Rings, Shapwick, Dorset

Ingpen = Inkpen Beacon, near Newbury, Berkshire

Inner Wessex = Dorset

The Island = Isle of Wight, Hampshire

Isles of Lyonesse = Scilly Isles, Cornwall

Isle of Slingers = Portland, Dorset

Ivel = Yeovil, Somerset

Ivel Way = Long Ash Lane (now the A37), from Dorchester and Stratton, Dorset, to Yeovil, Somerset

Ivelchester = Ilchester, Somerset

Ivell = Yeovil, Somerset

Jersey = itself, Jersey

Jordon Grove = itself, the Jordan Valley, Preston, near Weymouth

Keinton Mandeville = itself, Keinton Mandeville, Somerset

Kennetbridge = Newbury (on the River Kennet), Berkshire

King's Arms Inn, Casterbridge = itself, King's Arms Hotel, High East Street, Dorchester, Dorset

King's Hintock Court = Melbury House, Melbury Sampford, Dorset

King's Hintock Park = Melbury Park, Melbury Sampford, Dorset

Kingsbere = Bere Regis, Dorset

Kingsbere Hill = Black Hill, Bere Regis, Dorset

Kingsbere-sub-Greenhill = Bere Regis (beneath Woodbury Hill), Dorset

Knapwater House = Kingston Maurward House, Stinsford, Dorset

Knollingwood Hall = St Giles House, Wimborne St Giles, Dorset

Knollsea = Swanage, Dorset

Lambing Corner = itself, Lambing Corner between Caltford and Fyfield, near Marlborough, Wiltshire

Lane Inn, Stagfoot Lane = old Fox Inn, corner of Hartfoot Lane and Cothayes Drove, Lower Ansty, Dorset

Lanivet = itself, Lanivet, near Bodmin, Cornwall

Leddenton = Gillingham, Dorset

Lew Everard = West Stafford, Dorset

Lewgate = Higher Bockhampton, near Stinsford, Dorset

Little Enkworth = Kingston, near Corfe Castle, Dorset

Little Hintock = Stockwood and Hermitage, Dorset

Little Weatherbury Farm = Druce Farm, near Puddletown, Dorset

Little Welland = Winterborne Zelston, Dorset

Liverpool = itself, Liverpool

(The) Lookout, Budmouth = The Nothe, Weymouth, Dorset

London = itself, London

Long-Ash Lane = itself, Long Ash Lane (now the A37), Dorset

Longpuddle = Piddletrenthide, Dorset

Lord Quantock Arms, Markton = The Luttrell Arms, Dunster, Somerset

Lord's Barrow = itself, Lord's Barrow, West Chaldon, near Lulworth, Dorset

Lornton Inn = Horton Inn, near Horton, Dorset

Lower Longpuddle = Piddlehinton, Dorset

Lower Mellstock = Lower Bockhamton, near Stinsford, Dorset

Lower Wessex = Devon

Lulstead = West Lulworth, Dorset

Lulstead Cove = Lulworth Cove, West Lulworth, Dorset

Lulwind Cove = also Lulworth Cove, West Lulworth, Dorset

Lumsdon = Cumnor, near Oxford

Lydden Spring = itself, the source of the River Lydden, Buckland Newton, Dorset

Lyonnesse (Isles of) = Scilly Isles, Cornwall

Mai Dun = Maiden Castle, near Dorchester, Dorset

Maidon = also Maiden Castle, near Dorchester, Dorset

Manor Court = Rushmore House, Tollard Royal, Wiltshire

Market House, Casterbridge = Corn Exchange, North Square, Dorchester, Dorset

Market Place, Shaston = The Commons, Shaftesbury, Dorset

Markton = Dunster, Somerset

Marlbury = Marlborough, Wiltshire

Marlbury Downs = Marlborough Downs, Wiltshire

Marshcombe = Middlemarsh, Minterne Magna, Dorset

Marlott = Marnhull, Dorset

Marshal's Elm = itself, Marshall's Elm, near Street, Somerset

Marshwood = Middlemarsh, near Minterne Magna, Dorset

Martock Moor = itself, being the Somerset Levels near Martock, Somerset

Marygreen = Fawley, Berkshire

Max Gate = itself, Max Gate (originally Mack's Gate for its turnpike toll-house), Alington Avenue, Dorchester, Dorset

Melchester = Salisbury, Wiltshire

Melchester Cathedral = Salisbury Cathedral, Wiltshire

Mellstock = Stinsford, Dorset

Mellstock Cross = Stinsford Cross (between Lower Bockhampton and Higher Bockhampton), Stinsford, Dorset

Mellstock Lane = road east from Stinsford Hill to Stinsford Cross and Tincleton, Dorset

Mellstock Leaze = meadows (the Saxon word), south of Church Lane, Stinsford, Dorset

Mellstock Rise = Stinsford Hill (now with a roundabout on the A35), Stinsford, Dorset

Mendip = itself, the Mendip Hills, Somerset

Mid Wessex = Wiltshire

Middleton = Milton Abbas, Dorset

Middleton Abbey = Milton Abbey, Milton Abbas, Dorset

Millpond St Jude's = Milborne St Andrew, Dorset

Milton Wood = Delcombe Woods, Milton Abbas, Dorset

Mistover = Puddletown Heath, Puddletown, Dorset

Mistover Knap = Green Hill, south of Puddletown Beacon, Puddletown, Dorset

Mixen Lane, Durnover = Mill Street, Fordington. Dorset

Montislope = Montacute, Somerset

Moreford = Moreton, Dorset

Moreford Rise = Broomhill, Winfrith Newburgh, Dorset

Mount Lodge = Killerton House, Broadclyst, near Exeter, Devon

Mousehole = itself, Mousehole, near Penzance, Cornwall

Narrobourne = West Coker, near Yeovil, Somerset

Nest Cottage = Chine Hill Cottage (since demolished), Druce, near Puddletown, Dorset

Nether Moynton = Owermoigne, Dorset

Nether Wessex = Somerset

New Castle = Pennsylvania Castle, Wakeham, Portland, Dorset

New Parade, Solentsea = Clarence Parade, Southsea, Portsmouth, Hampshire
Nettlecombe Tout = itself, Nettlecombe Tout, Melcombe Horsey, Dorset
Newland Buckton = Buckland Newton, Dorset
Newton = Maiden Newton, Dorset
Nicholas Cottage = itself, St Nicholas Cottage, East Chaldon, Chaldon Herring, Dorset
Norcombe = Hooke or Toller Whelme, Dorset
Norcombe Hill = Winyard's Gap, Chedington, Dorset
North Wessex = Berkshire (particularly the part transferred to Oxfordshire in 1974)
North-West Avenue, Casterbridge = The Grove, Dorchester, Dorset
The Nothe, Budmouth = itself, The Nothe, Weymouth, Dorset
Nuttlebury = Hazelbury Bryan, Dorset
Nuzzlebury = also Hazelbury Bryan, Dorset

Oakbury Fitzpiers = Okeford Fitzpaine, Dorset
Oaker's Pool = itself, Oakers Pool, below Oakers Wood to the south of Briantspuddle, Dorset
Octagonal Chamber, Christminster = cupola of the Sheldonian Theatre, Oxford
Off-Wessex = Cornwall
Old Greyhound Inn, Casterbridge = itself, now Old Greyhound Yard, Dorchester, Dorset
Old Harry Rock(s) = itself, at Studland, Dorset
Old Melchester = Old Sarum, near Salisbury, Whiltshire
Old Rooms Inn, Budmouth = itself, the Old Rooms, Trinity Street, Weymouth, Dorset
Old Time Street, Christminster = Oriel Lane, Oxford
Oldgate College, Christminster = New College, Oxford
Oozewood = Ringwood, Hampshire
Oriel Window, Casterbridge = building in High West Street (replaced by the Buzz Inn), Dorchester, Dorset
Outer Wessex = Somerset
Overcombe = Sutton Poyntz, near Weymouth, Dorset
Overcombe Mill = Sutton Poyntz for the location with the actual mill buildings being based on Upwey Mill, near Weymouth, Dorset
Owlscombe = Batcombe, Dorset
Oxwell = Poxwell, Dorset
Oxwell Hall = Poxwell House, Poxwell, Dorset

Parret = itself, the River Parrett, Dorset and Somerset
Peakhill Cottage = Manor Gardens Cottage, Lower Bockhampton, near Stinsford, Dorset

Pebble Bank = Chesil Beach, Portland, Dorset

Pen-zephyr = Penzance, Cornwall

Peter's Finger, Durnover = former King's Head, Mill Street, Fordington, Dorchester, Dorset

Phoenix Inn, Casterbridge = itself, now Phoenix Court, High East Street, Dorchester, Dorset

Plymouth = itself, Plymouth, Devon

Port Bredy = Bridport, Dorset

Port Bredy Harbour = Bridport Harbour, West Bay, Dorset

Pos'ham = itself, being how the locals pronounce Portesham, Dorset

Priory Mill, Casterbridge = former Friary Mill, Friary Hill, Dorchester

Prospect Hotel = Hunter's Inn, Parracombe, near Coombe Martin, Devon

Puddle-sub-Mixen = Turners Puddle, Dorset

Pummery, Casterbridge = itself, being the former local name for Poundbury, Dorchester, Dorset

Pummery Tout, Casterbridge = Poundbury Camp, Poundbury, Dorchester, Dorset

Pure Drop Inn, Marlott = Crown Inn, Marnhull

Pydel Vale = Piddle Valley, upstream of Puddletown, Dorset

Quartershot = Aldershot Camp, Aldershot, Hampshire

Quiet Woman Inn [the building] = the old thatched Red Lion Inn at Winfrith Newburgh, Dorset (destroyed by fire on 13 May 1965, Fred Pitfield writes in *Hardy's Wessex Locations*) *Quiet Woman Inn* [the location] = former Wild Duck Inn (now Duck Dairy House), Duddle Heath, near Puddletown, Dorset

(The) Race = itself, the tidal Race, off Portland Bill, Dorset

Rainbarrow = itself, the prominent mound of the Rainbarrows cluster on Duddle Heath, Dorset

Red King's Castle = Bow and Arrow Castle (also known as Rufus Castle), Church Ope, Portland, Dorset

Red Lion Inn, Anglebury = itself, the Red Lion Hotel, West Street, Wareham, Dorset

Red Lion, Melchester = itself, the Red Lion Hotel, Milford Street, Salisbury, Wiltshire

Redrutin = Redruth, Cornwall

Revellers' Inn = former Revel's Inn (now Lower Revels Farm), Cosmore, Buckland Newton, Dorset

(The) Ridgeway = itself, on Ridgeway Hill, above Weymouth

Rimsmoor Pond = itself, Rimsmoor Pond, south of Briantspuddle, Dorset

(The) Ring, Casterbridge = Maumbury Ring, Dorchester, Dorset

Rings Hill = Weatherbry Castle hill-fort, Milborne St Andrew, Dorset

Rings Hill Speer = Hood Monument, Butleigh, Somerset

Ringsworth = Ringstead, Dorset

Rolliver's Alehouse, Marlott = former Lamb Inn (now Old Lamb House), Walton Elm Cross, Marnhull, though also attributed to the Blackmoor Vale Inn (now Blackmore Vale Inn), Burton Street, Marnhull, Dorset

Rook's Gate = entrance to Killerton Park, Broadclyst, near Exeter, Devon

Rookington House = Hurn Court (now Heron Court School), Hurn, Dorset

Rookington Park = Hurn Park, Hurn, Dorset

Round Pound = itself, Round Pound, Chaldon Down, near Lulworth, Dorset

Rou'tor Town = Bodmin (below Rough Tor), Cornwall

Roy Town = Troytown, Puddletown, Dorset

Rubdon Hill = Bubb Down Hill, Melbury Bubb, Dorset

Rubric College, Christminster = Brasenose College, Oxford

Rushy Pond = itself, Rushy Pond, Duddle Heath, near Puddletown, Dorset

St Clement's Isle = itself, St Clement's Isle, Mousehole, near Penzance, Cornwall

St James's, Havenpool = itself, St James's church, Poole, Dorset

St Launce's = Launceston, Cornwall

St Maria's = St Mary's, Isles of Scilly

St Mary's, Toneborough = itself, St Mary Magdalene church, Church Square, Taunton, Somerset

St Michael's Mount = itself, St Michael's Mount, Marazion, Cornwall

St Peter's Church = itself, St Peter's church, High West Street, Dorchester, Dorset

St Peter's Finger, Durnover = former King's Head, Mill Street, Fordington, Dorchester, Dorset

St Silas, Christminster = St Barnabas church (designed by Hardy's architectural associate Sir Arthur Blomfield), Oxford

St Thomas, Melchester = itself, the church of St Thomas Beckett, Salisbury, Wiltshire

(The) Sallows = riverside wood at Stafford House, West Stafford, Dorset

Sandbourne = Bournemouth (transferred from Hampshire to Bournemouth in 1974)

Sandbourne Moor = Bourne Bottom, Poole, Dorset

Sarcophagus College, Christminster = Corpus Christi College, Oxford

Scrimpton = Frampton, Dorset

Sedge-Moor = itself, the battlefield of Sedgemoor, Westonzoyland, Somerset

Shadwater = Woodsford, Dorset

Shadwater Weir = the River Frome at Woodsford Farm, Woodsford, Dorset

Shakeforest Towers = Clatford Hall, Fyfield, Marlborough, Wiltshire

Shaston = itself, Shaston, being the milestone contraction for Shaftesbury, Dorset

Sherton Abbas = Sherborne, Dorset

Sherton Abbas Castle = Sherborne (New) Castle, Sherborne, Dorset

Sherton Abbas Park = Sherborne Park, Sherborne, Dorset

Sherton Castle = Sherborne (Old) Castle, Sherborne, Dorset

Sherton Turnpike = West Hill Cottage, between Longburton and Sherborne, Dorset

Shottsford = Blandford, Dorset

Shottsford Forum = also Blandford Forum, Dorset

Sidlinch = Sydling St Nicholas, Dorset

Silverthorn Dairy = Up Exe, between Silverton and Thorverton, Devon

Sleeping Green = Withycombe, Somerset (with the Old King's Arms) or nearby Carhampton (with the Butchers' Arms)

The Slopes = foothills of Cranborne Chase, Dorset

Slopeway Well = Fortuneswell, Portland, Dorset

Slyer's Lane = itself, Slyer's Lane, Coker's Frome, near Stinsford, Dorset

Snail Creep = itself, Snail Creep being the local name for the path from Higher Bockhampton northwards to Grey's Wood, near Stinsford, Dorset

Solentsea = Southsea, Portsmouth, Hampshire

South Avon = River Avon, Wiltshire and Hampshire

South Wessex = Dorset

Southampton = itself, Southampton, Hampshire

Southerton = Stoborough

Sow-and-Acorn, Evershead = Acorn Inn, Evershot

Springham = Warmwell, Dorset

Stagfoot Lane = Hartfoot Lane, from Bingham's Melcombe to Lower Ansty, Dorset

(de) Stancy Castle = Dunster Castle, Dunster, Somerset

Standfast Bridge, Durnover = East Mills Bridge, Mill Lane, Fordington, Dorchester, Dorset

Stapleford = Stalbridge, Dorset

Stapleford Park = Stalbridge Park, Stalbridge, Dorset

Stickleford = Tincleton, Dorset

Stoke Barehills = Basingstoke, Hampshire

Stoke Lane = itself, Stoke Lane, between Mappowder and Stoke Wake, Dorset

Stonehenge = itself, Stonehenge, near Amesbury, Wiltshire

Stour = itself, the River Stour, Dorset (pronounced to rhyme with flower)

Stourcastle = Sturminster Newton, Dorset

Stourton Tower = Alfred's Tower, Brewham, Somerset

Street of Wells = High Street, Fortuneswell, Portland, Dorset

Sydling Mill = itself, the former Sydling Mill, Sydling St Nicholas, Dorset

Sylvania Castle = Pennsylvania Castle (now Pennsylvania Castle Hotel), Wakeham, Portland, Dorset

Talbothays Dairy = Lower Lewell Farm, West Stafford, Dorset

Talbothays Lodge = itself, Talbothays Lodge (designed by Thomas Hardy and built by Henry Hardy for their sister Kate), West Stafford, Dorset

Targan Bay = Pentargon Bay, near Boscastle, Cornwall

Ten Hatches = itself, the former Ten Hatches (now Coker's Frome Weir), on the River Frome near Stinsford, Dorset

Ten Hatches Hole, Casterbridge = itself, below the former Ten Hatches, Coker's Frome, Dorchester, Dorset

Tess's Cottage, Evershead = itself, Tess Cottage, up the hill on the west side of the parish church, Evershot, Dorset

Tess's Cottage, Marlott = Barton Cottage (now Tess Cottage), Walton Elm, Marnhull, Dorset

Tewnell Mill = Hooke Mill, Hooke, near Beaminster, Dorset

Theatre of Wren, Christminster = Sheldonian Theatre, Oxford

Thorncombe Wood, Mellstock = itself, Thorncombe Wood (beside Hardy's Cottage), Higher Bockhampton, near Stinsford, Dorset

Three Mariners' Inn, Casterbridge = itself, the former King of Prussia later known as the Three Mariners, High East Street (standing on the north side, east of Friary Lane), Dorchester, Dorset

Three Tranters' Inn = Wise Man Inn, West Stafford, Dorset

Throope Corner, Alderworth = junction at Throop Clump, Briantspuddle, Dorset

Tintinhull = itself, Tintinhull, near Montacute, Somerset

Tintinhull Valley = itself, at Tintinhull, beside Wellhams Brook below Stoke sub Hamdon, Somerset

Tivworthy = Tiverton, Devon

Tolchurch = Tolpuddle, Dorset

Toller Down = itself, Corscombe, Dorset

Toneborough = Taunton (on the River Tone), Somerset

Toneborough Barracks = Jellalabad Barracks, Mount Street, Taunton, Somerset

Toneborough Town Hall = the old Market House (now the Guildhall), Taunton, Somerset.

Toneborough Deane = Vale of Taunton Deane, Somerset

Tor-upon-Sea = Torquay, Devon

Town Bridge, Melchester = St Nicholas Bridge, Salisbury, Wiltshire

Town Hall, Casterbridge = Corn Exchange, North Square, Dorchester, Dorset

Town Hall, Havenpool = The Guilldhall, Poole, Dorset

Town Hall, Melchester = The Guildhall, Market Place, Salisbury, Wiltshire

Trantridge = Pentridge, Dorset

Travellers' Rest = itself, the Travellers' Rest Inn, near Shipton Gorge, Dorset

Trufal = Truro, Cornwall

Tudor College, Christminster = Brazenose College, Oxford

Turngate Street, Liverpool = an invented address

Tutcombe Bottom = Lewcombe, East Chelborough, Dorset

(The) Union, Casterbridge = itself, the former Union Workhouse, otherwise known as the Poor Law Institution, Damer's
   Road (facing junction with Maud Road), Dorchester, Dorset
Uplandtowers = St Giles House, Wimborne St Giles, near Cranborne, Dorset
Upper Longpuddle = Piddletrenthide, Dorset
Upper Mellstock = Higher Bockhampton, near Stinsford, Dorset
Upper Wessex = Hampshire
Upway Railway Station = itself, Upwey Station, near Weymouth, Dorset

Vagg Hollow = itself, Vagg Hollow below Vagg Farm, Vagg, north-west of Yeovil, Somerset
Valley of the Little Daries = Blackmore Vale, Dorset
Valley of the Great Daries = Frome Valley, Dorset
Vindilia = Portland, Dorset
Vindogladia = Woodyates, near Pentridge, Dorset

Waddon Vale = itself, Waddon, Portesham, Dorset
Warborne = Wimborne, Dorset
Wardour Castle = itself, Wardour Castle, near Tisbury, Wiltshire
Warm'ell Cross = itself, Warmwell Cross (now a roundabout), near Warmwell, Dorset
Waterstone Ridge = itself, Waterston Ridge, south of Lacock Dairy Farm, near Puddletown, Dorset
Weatherbury = Puddletown (known as Piddletown in Hardy's time), Dorset
Weatherbury Farm = Waterston Manor, between Piddlehinton and Puddletown, Dorset
Weatherbury Vicarage - itself, the former Vicarage, now Dawney House, Puddletown, Dorset
Welcome Home Inn, Castle Boterel = The Ship, The Harbour, Boscastle, Cornwall
Welland = Almer, near Sturminster Marshall, Dorset
Welland House = Charborough House, Morden, Dorset
Wellbridge = Wool Bridge, Wool, Dorset
Wellbridge Abbey = Bindon Abbey, Wool, Dorset
Wellbridge House = Woolbridge Manor, Wool, Dorset
Wellbridge Manor = also Woolbridge Manor, Wool, Dorset
Wellbridge Mill = Bindon Mill, Wool, Dorset
Wessex Heights = peaks of the Dorset Downs, plus those of Exmoor and the Quantock Hills, and eastwards to the
   Hampshire and Berkshire Downs
West Endelstow = St Juliot, near Boscastle, Cornwall
West Endelstow Church = St Julietta's Church, St Juliot, near Boscastle, Cornwall
West Poley = Priddy, near Wells, Somerset

West Walk, Casterbridge = West Walks, Dorchester, Dorset

Weydon Fair = Weyhill Fair, near Andover, Hampshire

Weydon Priors = Hurstbourne Priors, near Andover, Hampshire

Wherryborne = Winterborne Came, near Dorchester, Dorset

Wherryborne Rectory = Old Rectory (home of pastor-poet William Barnes), Winterborne Came, near Dorchester, Dorset

Wherryborne Wood = North Plantation, Came Park, Winterborne Came, near Dorchester, Dorset

Whit' Sheet Hill = itself, Whitesheet Hill, where Cromlech Crock Road (now the A356) ascends the downs from Maiden Newton, north of Toller Fratrum, Dorset

(The) White Hart, Melchester = itself, White Hart Hotel, St John's Street, Salisbury, Wiltshire

White Hart Tavern, Casterbridge = itself, White Hart Hotel, High East Street, Dorchester, Dorset

White Horse Inn, Chalk Newton = itself, the old White Horse Inn, Maiden Newton, Dorset

White Horse Inn, Hintock Green = itself, the former White Horse Inn (now the Hunter's Moon), Middlemarsh, Minterne Magna, Dorset

White-Hart Valley = Blackmore Vale

Windy Beak = Cambeak, St Gennys, near Bude, Cornwall

Windwhistle = itself, the Windwhistle Inn, near Crewkerne, Somerset

Wintoncester = Winchester, Hampshire

Wintoncester Cathedral = Winchester Cathedral, Winchester, Hampshire

Wolfeton House = itself, Wolfeton House, Charminster, Dorset

Woodyates Inn = itself, the former Woodyates Inn, Pentridge, Dorset

Woolcomb = itself, Woolcombe, near Evershot, Dorset

Wylls Neck = itself, Wills Neck, West Bagborough, Somerset

Wyndway House = Upton House, Poole, Dorset

Wynyard's Gap = itself, Winyard's Gap, near Chedington, Dorset

Yalbury Hill = Yellowham Hill, near Puddletown, Dorset

Yalbury Wood = Yellowham Wood, between Stinsford and Puddletown, Dorset

Yellowham Bottom = itself, the coombe on the west side of Yellowham Wood, near Stinsford, Dorset

Yewsholt Lodge = Farr's House, Cowgrove, near Pamphill, Dorset

Yeo = itself, the River Yeo, Dorset and Somerset